Securities & Investment Institute

Level 3

Certificate in Investments

Unit 2 – Securities and
Unit 4 – Securities and Financial Derivatives

Question Bank and Practice Examinations

November 2007

Syllabus version 8

BPP LEARNING MEDIA

Contents

ISBN: 9780 7517 4322 7

£65.00

Question Bank

Contents

1. Securities

Questions

1. **An investor, Mick, has an investment of £4,000 in a company consisting of 1,000 £2 nominal value fully paid-up shares. If the company went into liquidation, what is the most Mick could lose?**

   A Nothing further, as the shares are fully paid up

   B £1,000

   C £2,000

   D His loss is unlimited

---

2. **Which two of the following statements are not true with regard to warrants?**

   I Often issued as a 'sweetener' with a new share issue, particularly by investment trusts

   II Carry the right to vote at an Extraordinary General Meeting (EGM)

   III Do not carry the right to vote at the AGM or any other company meeting

   IV Carry the right to subscribe for new ordinary shares at the time and price of the investor's choice

   A I and IV

   B II and IV

   C III and IV

   D I and III

---

3. **Which of the following would best describe the rights of warrant holders?**

   A They can vote in a takeover bid

   B They have no voting rights

   C They have half the normal voting rights

   D They receive interest on the coupon

---

4. **A fully listed company, Anchor plc, has 'A' shares. What voting rights do they bestow upon shareholders?**

   A They carry voting rights equal to ordinary shares

   B They only have votes if dividends are passed

   C Two 'A' shares carry the same votes as one ordinary share

   D They carry no voting rights

5. Warrants on equity issues allow their owners

A To receive extra dividends on their shares

B To receive preferable treatment on liquidation

C To purchase additional shares at some date in the future if they choose to

D To declare their income to the tax authorities

6. Which of the following attributes might a warrant not have?

A An exercise price that may change during the life of the contract

B Protection against stock splits

C A shorter time to maturity at issue than a call option

D It may be attached to a bond issue

7. Which of the following is false concerning preference shares?

A They have no voting rights

B They are redeemable

C Their dividend is fixed

D Their dividend may be passed by the company

8. What currency is an ADR traded in?

A US dollars

B Sterling

C Australian dollars

D Yen

9. When do ADRs settle in the UK?

A T + 3

B T + 2

C T + 1

D No standard settlement

10. Which of the following are false of participating preference shares?

I Holders are entitled to increased dividends if the company's profits go above a certain level

II Holders are entitled to vote

III They rank below preferential creditors on liquidation

IV Holders are entitled to participate in rights issues

A II, III and IV

B II only

C II and IV

D II and III

11. When ADRs are issued pre-release, what type of collateral must be in place by the issuing bank?

A Gilts

B Cash

C Bonds

D Equities

---

12. All of the following are true of participating preference shares, except

A They receive dividends before ordinary shares

B They have pre-emptive rights over any new shares issued

C They rank below subordinated debt on liquidation

D They have a variable element of their dividend when profits of the company are above a certain level

---

13. Whilst reading the *Financial Times*, you notice that the gross redemption yield on a particular gilt-edged stock is greater than the flat interest yield. This means that the

A Market price is greater than par value

B Market price is less than par value

C Coupon is paid net

D Coupon is paid gross

---

14. Which of the following can be used to predict the change in the price of a bond, given the change in yield?

A Flat yield

B Gearing

C Gross redemption yield

D Modified duration

---

15. Indexation for gilt interest is based on the RPI for which period?

A Eight months prior to the date of issue to eight months prior to the payment date

B The date of issue to eight months prior to the payment date

C Eight months prior to the date of issue to the payment date

D The date of issue to the payment date

---

16. A bond is priced at £113.75 and has a modified duration of 3.45. If yields rise by ½%, what will the new price of the bond be?

A £94.15

B £111.79

C £115.71

D £133.35

17. All of the following are true of Eurobonds, except

A They are usually registered securities

B They are issued outside the country whose currency they are denominated in

C They are held in safe custody by Clearstream or Euroclear

D Interest on them is paid without any tax being deducted

---

18. Which of the following is true of a corporate debenture?

A It may be bearer stock

B Any charge must be registered with the Registrar of Companies

C It will be unsecured

D It cannot be convertible into equity

---

19. Which of the following bonds would be the most responsive to a shift of 1% in yields?

A Low coupon short dated

B Low coupon long dated

C High coupon short dated

D High coupon long dated

---

20. What is normal maturity of a T-bill?

A One month

B Three months

C Five months

D Six months

---

21. Which two of the following are true of a gilt trading below par?

I The gross redemption yield will exceed the flat yield

II The flat yield will exceed the gross redemption yield

III If held to maturity, the gilt will provide a capital gain

IV If held to maturity, the gilt will provide a capital loss

A I and III

B II and III

C I and IV

D II and IV

---

22. On a government stock dated 2014–2018, which of the following is true?

A Redemption must take place in 2014

B The government can redeem anytime between 2014 and 2018

C The stock will be index linked

D The government can redeem at any time if the coupon is less than interest rates

23. Which of the following government bonds pay interest annually?

A UK

B US

C Japan

D Germany

---

24. What would be the order of priority on liquidation for the following?

I Employee's wage arrears

II Loans secured by a fixed charge

III Preferential shareholders

IV Trade creditors

A I, III, II, IV

B II, I, IV, III

C I, II, III, IV

D I, II, IV, III

---

25. Most Japanese government bonds (JGBs) are issued with maturities of

A 10 years

B 15 years

C 20 years

D 25 years

---

26. Which of the following statements is true with respect to Treasury bills?

A They are normally issued with a life of 183 days

B They are issued at a discount to face value

C The minimum denomination for a sterling bill is £50,000

D They are only available to the Discount Houses

---

27. If you buy £100,000 of the 3½% War Loan on 1 September for £72, how much income will be received on 1 December?

A £1,750

B £3,500

C £17,500

D £35,000

---

28. Gilts that are classified as longs have what minimum period to run to redemption?

A 10 years

B 15 years

C 20 years

D 25 years

29. If interest rates increase, which of the following statements would be true for gilts?

A Prices would rise and yields would fall

B Prices would rise and yields would rise

C Prices would fall and yields would rise

D Prices would fall and yields would fall

30. If a UK private investor has elected for a withholding tax on his gilt interest and holds £100,000 of Treasury 7% 2010, which has a current interest yield of 7.10% and a market value of £98,500, what amount will he receive at the next coupon date, assuming he held the stock for the entire interest period?

A £5,600

B £3,500

C £2,800

D £2,840

31. Which of the conditions noted below are least likely to be true for Eurobond issues?

A They are bearer securities

B They are normally sold by a syndicate of international banks

C They are largely placed with retail investors

D They are mostly cleared through Euroclear and Clearstream

32. Which is the normal style of coupon payment for gilts?

A Annually gross

B Annually net of basic rate tax

C Semi-annually net of basic rate tax

D Semi-annually gross

33. Which of the following would have the highest modified duration?

A Long-dated and high-coupon bonds

B Long-dated and low-coupon bonds

C Short-dated and high-coupon bonds

D Short-dated and low-coupon bonds

34. Which of the following is not true of US T-bonds?

A They have a life of over 20 years

B They always pay coupons

C They are registered instruments

D They are the US equivalent of the UK gilt

35. If interest rates are expected to fall, what effect will this have on a holding of Treasury 6¼% 2010?

I Price will rise

II Yield will fall

III Price will fall

IV Yield will rise

A I and IV

B I and II

C II and III

D III and IV

36. Which of the following bonds pays a semi-annual coupon?

A French government bonds

B German government bonds

C Japanese government bonds

D Eurobonds

37. What is a yield curve?

A A plot of the gross redemption yields of bonds with various maturities at a point in time

B A plot of the gross redemption yields of bonds with various maturities over time

C A graph of an index of bonds of different maturities plotted over time

D The plot of an index of bonds' accrued interest over time

38. Which of the following is the normal life of the French government bond, known as the OAT?

A 20 years

B Between seven and 30 years

C Up to ten years

D Over ten years

39. What is the real yield on a bond held for the last year?

A Nominal yield less expected inflation

B Nominal yield plus expected inflation

C Actual inflation for the last year

D Nominal yield less actual inflation for the last year

40. What is the maturity of the Japanese 'superlong' bond?

A 5 years

B 15 years

C 20 years

D 10 years

41. An inverted yield curve reflects the expectation that

A Short-term interest rates will rise

B Long-term interest rates will fall

C Short-term interest rates will fall

D Long-term interest rates will rise

42. A long and short-dated gilt both have a market price of 90. If interest rates increase, which of the following statements is true?

A The short-gilt price will increase more than the long-gilt price

B The long-gilt price will increase more than the short-gilt price

C The short-gilt price will fall more than the long-gilt price

D The long-gilt price will fall more than the short-gilt price

43. If a gilt has a maturity of 2010-2017 and a coupon of 10% and current interest rates are 5%, which of the following statements is true?

A The DMO would immediately buy the gilt in the market place to reissue at cheaper rates

B The DMO will aim to redeem the gilt at the earliest opportunity

C The DMO will aim to redeem the gilt at the latest possible opportunity

D The DMO will be indifferent as to any of the above courses of action

44. A convertible was issued several years ago at £103 per £100 of nominal value with the right to subscribe for 30 shares. The existing share price is £3 and the market price of the convertible is £95. What is the conversion premium?

A 3.0%

B 5.6%

C 11.1%

D 14.4%

45. You are advising a charity on a long-term investment in the UK Gilt market. Which would be the most relevant criterion to base the decision on?

A The flat yield

B The net redemption yield

C The gross redemption yield

D The grossed-up net redemption yield

46. The London Stock Exchange's definition of a short-dated gilt is one that

A Has a remaining life of five years or less

B Was issued with a remaining life of seven years or less

C Has a remaining life of seven years or less

D Was issued with a remaining life of five years or less

47. All of the following characterise Eurobonds and the Eurobond market, except

A An international market

B Bonds issued in bearer form

C New issues that are usually syndicated

D The majority of investors being high net worth individuals

---

48. What does the term convexity describe?

A The volatility of bond prices given a change in interest rates

B The actual relationship between bond prices and interest rates is curved rather than linear

C The inverse price relationship

D The net yield required from a bond to compensate for inflation

---

49. Calculate the current value of a £100 nominal value holding of a bond with an annual coupon of 5% if it matures in two years' time. Interest rates are expected to remain at 4.5% over the period.

A £100

B £100.93

C £99.07

D £105.48

---

50. Calculate the present value of the second year's annual coupon on a £100 nominal value holding of a 6% bond when interest rates are 4%.

A £6.00

B £5.92

C £6.48

D £5.55

---

51. What is the normal maturity of the US T-bond on issue?

A 2-10 years

B 2-5 years

C 5-10 years

D More than 10 years

---

52. When does a trade in the BOBL settle?

A T + 1

B T + 2

C T + 3

D T + 5

53. What does the yield curve show?

A Price against time

B Price against maturity

C Yield against maturity

D Price against yield

---

54. Which of the following range of bond maturities is not correct ?

A US T-Bond: >10 years

B Japanese Superlong Bond: 20 years

C BOBL: <10 years

D Schatz: 2 years

---

55. An investor owns £10,000 of an 8% bond which is currently priced at 200p. The bond pays annual income. Calculate how much income they will receive at the next income payment date.

A £1,600

B £800

C £1,200

D £400

---

56. Which of the following are true of Eurobonds?

I They are in bearer form throughout their lives

II They have a fixed or determinable interest rate

III They all have variable redemption dates

IV They must be US dollar denominated

A I and II

B I and III

C I, II and IV

D I, II, III and IV

---

57. Settlement for foreign currency spot deals is usually

A One business day

B Two business days

C Three business days

D The day agreed by the participants to the transaction

---

58. Which of the following is true with respect to the currency market?

A Trading is by open outcry in a formalised market place

B Spot trades are those which settle on a future date agreed between the two counterparties

C Forward rates represent the market's estimate of future spot rates

D Most currencies are quoted against the US dollar

59. If the spot rate for cable is $1.9770-$1.9860 and the forward rate is 0.36-0.35c pm, at what forward rate will the bank sell US dollars?

A $1.9895

B $1.9825

C $1.9736

D $1.9734

60. Forward foreign exchange contracts are usually settled

A One month after the date of the transaction

B Three months after the day of the transaction

C Six months after the day of the transaction

D At a date agreed by the participants to the transaction

61. If the US dollar to sterling rate was quoted in London as USD1.9770-USD1.9850, how many dollars would you receive for £1m?

A $503,778

B $505,817

C $1,977,000

D $1,985,000

62. If the US dollar was quoted at a premium of 0.5-0.4 to sterling on the forward foreign exchange markets in the UK, then the forward quote should be

A Added to the spot rate

B Deducted from the spot rate

C The same as the spot rate

D Not determinable from such information

63. Which two of the following are true of the UK currency market?

I Only spot transactions are possible

II Default risk is carried by the International Currency Clearing House

III There is no formal market place

IV Transactions will be frequently undertaken through a currency broker

A II and IV

B I and IV

C I and III

D III and IV

64. Which of the following regulates the Eurobond market?

A ICMA

B AIBD

C IPMA

D Clearstream

65. Which of the following is true of the Eurobond market?

A The market is regulated by ICMA

B Trades must be reported into TRAX by the end of the business day of the trade

C Settlement via the clearing houses Euroclear and Clearstream takes place three calendar days after the trade date

D Settlement can take place between Clearstream and Euroclear by using the electronic information link known as SPAN

66. When would you normally pay for a gilt following purchase?

A London Stock Exchange settlement day

B Five working days after the trade

C Same day

D Next business day

67. When dealing in UK debenture stock, when would you normally expect to settle the bargain?

A Three business days hence

B Two days hence

C The next day

D On account day

68. The FTSE 100 index comprises the 100 largest companies measured by reference to

A Revenue

B Market capitalisation

C Turnover

D Share price

69. A fund consisting of mainly top continental European shares is best measured against a benchmark of

A Eurotrack 100

B FTSE All Share

C DAX

D S&P 500

BPP LEARNING MEDIA

70. The Dow Jones Industrial Average is based on

A The prices of all stocks traded on the New York Stock Exchange

B The prices of the largest 100 stocks traded on the New York Stock Exchange

C Only industrial companies which have been quoted on the New York Stock Exchange since 1928

D The prices of the largest 30, industrial, blue chip stocks traded on the New York Stock Exchange

---

71. To which of the following markets does the Hang Seng Index relate?

A Osaka

B Tokyo

C Hong Kong

D Singapore

---

72. The main services offered by a Prime Broker to its hedge fund clients include which of the following?

I Core settlement

II Leverage trade execution

III Global custody including clearing and asset servicing

IV Investment decision making on behalf of client

A I only

B I and II

C I, II and III

D I, II, III and IV

---

73. Which of the following is not an equity financing method employed by Prime Brokers on behalf of their hedge fund clients?

A Rehypothecation

B Stock borrowing and lending

C An offer for sale

D Repo agreements

---

74. Which of the following is the correct priority on liquidation, from first to last?

I Debenture

II Ordinary share

III Preference share

IV Unsecured loand

A I, II, III, IV

B II, III, I, IV

C I, IV, III, II

D III, II, I, IV

75. **Based on the following information, what will the ordinary shareholders receive from the liquidator upon winding up?**

A company is put into liquidation and has assets available for pay-out of £975,000. The company has the following creditors.

	£
Liquidator's expenses	25,000
Tax authorities	150,000
Fixed charge holders	250,000
Trade creditors	400,000

The company has in issue £100,00 nominal of 10% preference shares in respect of which a dividend has been neither declared, nor paid, for the last five years. There are 200,000 ordinary £1 shares.

A Nothing

B 25p per share

C 50p per share

D The £1 nominal value of the share

76. **On the liquidation of an investment trust, in what order would the following rank (highest ranking first)?**

I Zero-coupon preference shares

II Unsecured loan stock

III Income shares

IV Debenture capital

A I, II, IV, III

B IV, I, III, II

C IV, II, I, III

D IV, II, III, I

Answers

1. **A** Mick's liability is limited to the nominal value of the shares. As the shares are fully paid up, he would have no further liability

   See Section 1 of your Study Book

2. **B** They carry no voting rights whatsoever. The exercise price is set at the outset, not at the investor's choice

   See Section 5 of your Study Book

3. **B** Warrant holders do not have a right to vote. Warrants give the right to buy new shares at a specified price on some date in the future

   See Section 5 of your Study Book

4. **D** 'A' Shares do not carry any voting rights

   See Section 2.2.1 of your Study Book

5. **C** Warrants are options on new issues, allowing investors to increase their holdings at specified 'strike' prices at noted dates in the future

   See Section 5 of your Study Book

6. **C** The exercise price will be changed if the company does a bonus or rights issue or stock split during the life of the warrant. Call options on Euronext.liffe last up to nine months, whereas warrants will usually be for several years

   See Section 5 of your Study Book

7. **B** The dividend may not be paid, but would normally be paid cumulatively in arrears thereafter. Preference shareholders will only get the right to vote if the shares are not paid for five years. Preference shares would not normally be redeemable

   See Section 3.1 of your Study Book

8. **A** American Depository Receipts (ADRs) trade on both the NYSE and LSE in US dollars

   See Section 4 of your Study Book

9. **A** The settlement period is the same as for equities

   See Section 4 of your Study Book

10. **C** Even participating preference shares do not have voting rights or the chance to take part in rights issues

    See Section 3.2 of your Study Book

11. **B** The collateral must be cash

    See Section 4 of your Study Book

12. **B** As their name suggests, they are given preferential treatment when it comes to the payment of dividends, i.e. they get paid before ordinary shareholders. Statement B is incorrect, since pre-emption rights are there to protect the voting rights of shareholders and since preference shares do not normally carry voting rights, they do not require pre-emption rights

See Section 3.2 of your Study Book

13. **B** The gilt is priced at less than par as there will be a capital gain on redemption. This is why the redemption yield is greater than the flat yield

See Section 12 of your Study Book

14. **D** This is the only one that measures volatility. The higher the modified duration, the higher a bond's volatility with respect to changes in yield

See Section 13.2 of your Study Book

15. **A** There is an eight-month time lag to enable accrued interest to be calculated during the six-month coupon period

See Section 15.1 of your Study Book

16. **B** $\Delta P = -MD \times \Delta Y \times \text{Price}$

Price change: $-3.45 \times 0.005 \times £113.75 = -£1.96$

New price: £113.75 – £1.96 = £111.79

See Section 13.2 of your Study Book

17. **A** They are bearer securities paying an annual gross coupon

See Section 19.1 of your Study Book

18. **B** A debenture carries both a fixed and floating charge

See Sections 17.2.1 and 17.2.2 of your Study Book

19. **B** The bond with the highest modified duration, as it has a low coupon and is long dated and is therefore the most volatile

See Section 13.1.1 of your Study Book

20. **B** Three months or 91 calendar days to be precise. The DMO (**not** Bank of England) do issue T-bills with maturities of one month and six months, but the most common issue is for three months

See Section 18.2 of your Study Book

21. **A** If you buy a gilt below par (e.g. for £95), you will make a capital gain when you receive the £100 nominal value on redemption. This gain will be added onto the coupon to give a higher GRY than the FY

See Section 10 of your Study Book

22. **B** The Government has the choice to redeem the stocks between the two dates that have been specified. They will normally do this if the coupon is higher than interest rates

See Section 10 of your Study Book

23. **D** All the others usually pay interest semi-annually

See Section 9 of your Study Book

24. **B** The wages owed to employees of the insolvent company would be a preferential creditor, ranking below fixed charge holders

See Section 1 of your Study Book

25. **A** Japanese government bonds (JGBs) may have a maturity of ten or 20 years, but the norm is ten years

See Section 16 of your Study Book

26. **B** Normal life is 91 days with a minimum denomination of £25,000. Anyone may trade in treasury bills. As they do not pay any interest, they trade below the par value

See Section 9 of your Study Book

27. **A** Gilts pay a coupon semi-annually as a percentage of the nominal value purchased. We must assume from the question that 1 December is the next coupon date. The investor is purchasing cum div and will receive all of the next coupon

£100,000 nominal value × 3.5% annual coupon × 0.5 = £1,750

See Section 10.3 of your Study Book

28. **B** This is the same whether we are using the official classification (DMOs) or the FT/LSE classification. Remember, as a general rule when you are not told which classification to use, then you should use the DMO's version

See Section 10.2 of your Study Book

29. **C** Yields move in line with interest rates, but prices move inversely to interest rates

See Section 13.1.1 of your Study Book

30. **C**

		£	
Annual interest =	7% × £100,000 =	7,000	gross
Six-monthly =	½ × £7,000 =	3,500	gross
Less 20% tax		(700)	
Receipt (net)		2,800	

See Section 10.3 of your Study Book

31. **C** Eurobonds tend to be aimed at the professional wholesale investor

See Section 1.9.1 of your Study Book

32. **D** This is generally true, unless an individual has elected for 20% tax to be deducted at source

See Section 10.3 of your Study Book

33. **B** High modified duration means high volatility. The bond with the lowest coupon fixed for the longest time will suffer the greatest fall in price if interest rates rise

See Section 13.2 of your Study Book

34. **A** Overseas government bonds are frequently examined. US T-notes are medium-term bonds (two to ten years) with T-bonds being long dated (over ten years). They are very similar to gilts, i.e. they settle T + 1, are registered and pay semi-annual coupons

See Section 16 of your Study Book

35. **B** There is an inverse relationship between gilt prices and interest rates. When interest rates go down, this means that gilt prices will go up. If gilt prices go up, the yield on the gilt will fall

See Section 13.1.1 of your Study Book

36. **C** The others are annual

See Section 16 of your Study Book

37. **A** A yield curve is a 'snapshot' at one particular point in time

See Section 14 of your Study Book

38. **B** The French OAT has a normal life of between seven and 30 years. The JGB has ten years normally or 'superlongs' with lives of 20 years. The German Bund has a life of up to ten years, and the US 'T'-bond has a life of over ten years

See Section 16 of your Study Book

39. **D** The nominal return from a bond is the real return plus an allowance to reflect inflation

See Section 15.1 of your Study Book

40. **C** The 'normal' life is ten years, while superlongs have a life of 20 years

See Section 16 of your Study Book

41. **C** An inverted yield curve is where the short-term rates are high, but the market anticipates that this cannot last for long, therefore the short-term interest rates are expected to fall. Technically, long-term interest rates may also be falling, but C is the best available answer

See Section 14.2 of your Study Book

42. **D** Longer dated stock is more volatile. If interest rates increase, the gilt price will fall

See Section 13.1.1 of your Study Book

43. **B** Assuming interest rates remain below the coupon rate, the Debt Management Office (DMO) will redeem as soon as possible to replace with a lower coupon issue

See Section 10.2 of your Study Book

44. **B** $\frac{\text{£95}}{\text{30 shares}}$ = £3.17 per share, a premium of 17p over the price of £3

$$\frac{\text{17p}}{\text{£3}} \times 100 = 5.6\%$$

Note that the issue price is irrelevant

See Section 17.5 of your Study Book

BPP LEARNING MEDIA

45. **C** Since the gross redemption yield is a measure of total return before taxation, and since charities do not pay tax, this would be the best available answer

See Section 12.2 of your Study Book

46. **A** Note that the official classification would be the Debt Management Office classification of a gilt having less than seven years to maturity. The London Stock Exchange and the *Financial Times* classify short-dated gilts as having less than five years until maturity

See Section 10.2 of your Study Book

47. **D** Eurobonds are normally bearer instruments which pay a gross dividend. It is normally institutions that buy Eurobonds

See Section 19 of your Study Book

48. **B** Convexity is the term used to reflect the actual relationship between bond prices and interest rates which is curved, not linear

See Section 13.3 of your Study Book

49. **B**

$$\text{Present value} = \frac{CF_1}{(1+r)} + \frac{CF_2}{(1+r)^2}$$

$$= \frac{£5}{1.045} + \frac{£105}{(1.045)^2}$$

$$= £4.78 + £96.15 = £100.93$$

See Section 11.3 of your Study Book

50. **D** Annual coupon = £100 n.v. × 6% = £6

$$\text{Present value} = \frac{CF_2}{(1+r)^2}$$

$$= \frac{£6}{(1+0.04)^2} = £5.55$$

See Section 11.3 of your Study Book

51. **D** T-bonds have a minimum maturity of 10 years

See Section 16 of your Study Book

52. **C** Standard settlement for German Government Debt is T+3

See Section 16 of your Study Book

53. **C** The yield curve shows how the yields of bonds of a similar class vary according to the bonds' maturity

See Section 14 of your Study Book

54. **C** BOBLs have maturities of up to five years, rather than up to ten. Although (given that five is lower than ten) you could say that the statement in C is not technically 'incorrect', it must be the one to go for because the other answers are indisputably 'correct'

See Section 16 of your Study Book

55. **B** Please note that the bond is paying income ANNUALLY, so the calculation is simply £10,000 x 0.08 = £800. The price of 200p seems slightly odd but remember the price has no relevance to the calculation of interest

See Section 10.3 of your Study Book

56. **A** Eurobonds need not be $ denominated and may be in 'bullet form' (i.e. with a fixed redemption date)

See Section 12 of your Study Book

57. **B** T + 2 is how it is usually described. A forward exchange rate transaction would be settled on the day agreed by the participants of the transaction

See Section 20.2 of your Study Book

58. **D** There is no formal market place for the currency markets – trades are conducted by screen and over the telephone. Spot trades settle T + 2, while forward trades settle on a date agreed between the two counterparties. Forward rates tend to represent the market's view on future interest rates, not future spot rates. Consequently, D remains the only answer option that is true – most currencies are indeed quoted against the US dollar

See Section 19.1 of your Study Book

59. **D** Subtract a premium (pm) from the spot to get the forward

$1.9770	–	$1.9860
($0.0036)	–	($0.0035)
$1.9734		$1.9825

The bank buys £1 for $1.9734 and sells £1 for $1.9825, i.e. the banks sells for $1.9734. Alternatively, you could turn the question around to say that, if the bank is selling dollars, the investor is buying dollars. When the investor is buying dollars, they receive the lower (or worst) amount

See Section 20.3.2 of your Study Book

60. **D** Remember that spot transactions settle T + 2

See Section 20.2 of your Study Book

61. **C** £1,000,000 × $1.9770 = $1,977,000. The left-hand (lower) rate is the dollar buying rate

See Section 20.3.2 of your Study Book

62. **B** Where the quote is direct, then the premium is deducted. It is the dollar trading at a premium to sterling

See Section 20.3.2 of your Study Book

63. **D** Spot and forward currency transactions are both common in the UK currency market. Whilst there is no formal market place, it is true to say that most transactions will be undertaken through a currency broker

See Section 20 of your Study Book

64. **A** The International Capital Markets Association (ICMA)

See Section 19.1 of your Study Book

65. **A** The market is regulated by the International Capital Market Association (ICMA). Trades must be input into TRAX within 30 minutes of the trade. Settlement will take place three **business** days after the trade date. The electronic information link between Clearstream and Euroclear is known as the Bridge

See Section 19.1 of your Study Book

66. **D** T + 1 is the settlement date for a gilt

See Section 11 of your Study Book

67. **A** Corporate bond settlement conforms to the international settlement convention of T + 3

See Section 9.2 of your Study Book

68. **B** FTSE 100 is the top 100 UK companies by market capitalisation (Share price × Number of shares)

See Section 8.2 of your Study Book

69. **A** The other indices only relate to one country's shares

See Section 7.2 of your Study Book

70. **D** The Dow Jones is based on 30 companies only

See Section 8.2 of your Study Book

71. **C** It is essential to learn the indices and the markets to which they relate

See Section 8.2 of your Study Book

72. **C** Prime Brokers do not make investment decisions for their clients

See Section 21 of your Study Book

73. **C** An offer for sale is an option for issuing shares on a stock exchange via the primary market. It is not an equity financing service offered by a Prime Broker

See Section 21.1 of your Study Book

74. **C** Ordinary shareholders are ranked below the others on liquidation. A debenture is a secured loan

See Section 17.3 of your Study Book

75. **B**

	£
Assets	975,000
External creditors	(825,000)
Nominal value preference shares	(100,000)
	50,000

No. of ordinary shares 200,000

Amount per share $\frac{£50{,}000}{200{,}000} = 25p$

As the preference dividend was never declared, the preference shareholders are not entitled to dividend arrears

See Section 17.3 of your Study Book

76. **C** Debt is paid first, then equity. Zero-dividend preference shares (zeros) are paid before any other type of equity

See Section 17.3 of your Study Book

2. New Issues of Securities

Questions

1. **What is a stag?**

   A Someone who buys new issues for short-term profit

   B A long-term investor

   C An investor who has a neutral view of market volatility

   D An investor who wishes to reduce CGT liabilities

---

2. **Which is true of a scrip issue?**

   A The shares are issued for at least nominal value

   B It is an issue to shareholders pro rata their shareholdings

   C Cash is raised by the issuer

   D It is a flotation

---

3. **All of the following are the same, except for**

   A Scrip issues

   B Capitalisation issues

   C Open issues

   D Bonus issues

---

4. **Which of the following share issues would not normally be underwritten?**

   A Placing

   B Deep discounted rights issue

   C Open offer

   D Offer for subscription

---

5. **When a company utilises reserves to make a share issue that does not raise funds, which of the following terms is not a usual description of such an issue?**

   A Bonus issue

   B Rights issue

   C Scrip issue

   D Capitalisation issue

6. Which of the following is not a marketing operation?

A Rights issue

B Introduction

C Open offer

D Offer for sale

7. All of the following are rules that apply to a company applying for a listing through the UKLA, except

A Minimum market capitalisation of shares must be £200,000

B Minimum three years' trading history

C At least 25% of shares available for trading publicly

D Shares freely transferable

8. Alpha plc and Beta plc have identical operations. Alpha plc has a significantly lower free float. In identical trading conditions, the shares of Alpha are, compared to Beta, most likely to experience

A An increase in volatility

B A decrease in volatility

C Identical performance

D No similarities other than coincidental

9. Which of the following is most at risk for the underwriter if it cannot fully distribute the underwritten issue? The underwriter's

A Subordinated stock

B Fixed income debt

C Equity

D Cash

10. All of the following are advantages accruing to a company as a result of having its shares listed on the LSE, except

A Access to public funds via the issue of shares

B The prestige given as a result of obtaining a quote which could assist trading prospects

C The short-term view of the management of the company that may result from the behaviour of institutional investors

D The ability to take over another company using only shares as consideration

11. Which two of the following are normally true of underwriting fees?

I Based on total number of shares
II Based on total value of shares
III Based on proportion remaining unsold
IV Regardless of proportion remaining unsold

A I and III
B I and IV
C II and III
D II and IV

12. Which of the following is the most closely linked to "free float"?

A Market capitalisation
B Share price
C Shareholders' funds
D Authorised share capital

13. What is false about open offers?

A Issued pro rata to existing holdings
B Can be sold nil-paid
C Means of raising cash for company
D Will involve a common subscription price

14. Which of the following may need to be underwritten?

A Bonus Issue
B Rights Issue
C Capitalisation issue
D Scrip issue

15. A company buys back its own shares on the market and holds them without cancelling them. How will the market cap of the company be affected?

A Increase
B Decrease
C Stay the same
D Indeterminable

16. Which best describes the role of a co-lead manager in a Eurobond issue?

A Arranging roadshows
B Underwriting the issue
C Communicating instructions
D Assisting the lead manager with the logistics of marketing the issue

17. How are underwriters' fees most likely to be determined?

A Based on the total value of shares underwritten

B Based on the total number of shares underwritten

C Based on the value of unsold shares

D Based on the number of unsold shares

Answers

1. **A** Stock market terminology for someone looking to make a quick profit on a new issue of shares. The privatisation issues of the 1980s and 1990s had many stags

   See Section 4.8.1 of your Study Book

2. **B** Another term for a bonus issue, also known as a capitalisation issue or scrip issue

   See Section 6.1 of your Study Book

3. **C** An open issue is a type of rights issue

   See Section 6.1 of your Study Book

4. **B** The deeper the discount that the rights price is to the current share price, the more likely investors are to subscribe

   See Section 6.3 of your Study Book

5. **B** A rights issue is used to raise new funds

   See Section 5 of your Study Book

6. **B** Introductions do not result in finance being raised from the share issue and therefore this is not a marketing operation

   See Section 4.9 of your Study Book

7. **A** The minimum market capitalisation for shares is £700,000. The minimum capitalisation for debt is £200,000

   See Section 2.1 of your Study Book

8. **A** Free float relates to the amount of a company's share capital that is available for trading by members of the public. If there are less shares in Alpha available to buy and sell, its share price will be more volatile. Since free float has an impact on the potential volatility of the share price, it is worth noting that FTSE Indices are weighted according to free float

   See Section 2.1.1 of your Study Book

9. **D** The underwriter will have an obligation to purchase any shares not taken up in the original offer. In the event that this obligation is realised, it would impact on the cash required to finance the purchase

   See Section 6.3 of your Study Book

10. **C** A listing is a way that a company can raise funds via the issue of shares. Gaining a listing may assist trading prospects by increasing the liquidity of the share, especially if the share is listed on the Full List. Being able to take over a company using only shares as consideration, rather than cash, means that a company can expand without needing to raise finance

    See Section 1 of your Study Book

11. **D** Underwriters generally retain their fees regardless of the number of unsold shares they are actually required to take up. The value, rather than number, of shares in the issue will determine the level of fees

See Section 6.3 of your Study Book

12. **A** In some contexts 'Market Capitalisation' and 'Free Float' are used synonymously. Market Capitalisation can mean the total market value of all the company's shares in issue, whereas Free Float means the total value of those shares freely traded on the market. However, the two terms are very closely related

See Section 2.1.1 of your Study Book

13. **B** Open offers are non-renounceable. This means that existing shareholders either take up the right to buy new shares, or refuse, but cannot sell the opportunity on to other investors

See Section 5.3 of your Study Book

14. **B** This is the only one of the four which is designed to raise finance. However, if the rights issue were deeply discounted, it would be very unlikely to require underwriting

See Section 5 of your Study Book

15. **B** Market capitalisation includes only those shares in issue, so the shares bought back will be excluded regardless of whether the company cancels them or holds them in Treasury

See Section 2.1.1 of your Study Book

16. **D** The other answers may be specific parts of the co-lead manager's role, but this is the best overall description

See Section 6.5.2 of your Study Book

17. **A** Fees are payable regardless of how much of the issue the underwriter actually has to take up

See Section 6.3 of your Study Book

3. Primary and Secondary Markets

Questions

1. **All of the following can be traded on the London Stock Exchange, except**

   A Gilts
   B Corporate debentures
   C Equity
   D Index derivatives

2. **Which of the following is the system to confirm transactions in Eurobonds?**

   A Euroclear
   B The Bridge
   C Clearstream
   D TRAX

3. **Which two of the following statements are generally true of both limit and execute and eliminate orders?**

   I They can be entered during call periods
   II They will state a limit price
   III They can be matched during the uncrossing period
   IV They can achieve price improvement

   A III and IV
   B II and IV
   C II and III
   D I and IV

4. **With reference to the SETS order book below, at what price will an incoming order to sell 5,000 shares at best be matched?**

	Buy			Sell			
	Time	Volume	Price	Price	Volume	Time	
A	09:41	1,700	855	857	3,500	08:55	D
B	09:58	4,300	855	858	1,000	09:15	E
C	09:57	1,400	854	860	2,300	10:25	F

   A 857.5
   B 854
   C 856
   D 855

5. **Which of the following best describes the role of committed principals in the International Retail Service?**

A They regulate the London Stock Exchange

B They ensure the timely settlement of trades between members

C They are institutional clients who are obliged to quote firm prices to each other

D They are market makers who are obliged to quote firm prices during the Mandatory Quote Period

6. **An order is placed on the SETS order book to buy 5,000 shares limit 757, fill or kill. The order book is shown below. How will this order be dealt with by SETS?**

	Buy			Sell			
	Time	Volume	Price	Price	Volume	Time	
A	09:41	1,700	755	757	3,500	08:55	D
B	09:58	4,300	755	758	1,000	09:15	E
C	09:57	1,400	754	760	2,300	10:25	F

A Fill 3,500 at 757 and the remainder eliminated

B Fill 3,500 at 757 with the remainder added to the top of the buy side of the order book.

C Fill 3,500 at 757, 1,000 at 758 and 500 at 760

D Whole order will be eliminated

7. **On which of the following trading platforms do most AIM shares trade?**

A SEAQ

B SETS

C SETSqx

D SETSmm

8. **All of the following orders can be partially filled, except**

A Limit order

B Fill or kill order

C Market order

D At best order

9. **Which of the following is false of TRAX?**

A It can be used for trade reporting

B It can be used for transaction reporting

C It can be used to communicate with Euroclear

D It is mainly used for Eurobonds

10 Using the information below, in order to satisfy FSA principles of best execution, the firm must execute the order at a price no worse than what amount?

Buy Orders		Sell Orders	
Volume	**Price**	**Price**	**Volume**
3,700	755	757	6,000
1,400	755	758	8,200
9,300	754	760	12,100

The order book above shows the state of the order book in a SETS security at 11:00. At this time, a firm wishes to execute an order to sell 5,000 shares away from the order book. At the same time, a separate telephone trade takes place in that security to sell 50,000 shares at 756. Details of these trades are printed on the market ticker.

A 754

B 755

C 756

D 757

---

11. Which of the following is true of virt-x?

A Publishes trades instantly on the virt-x system

B Is the responsibility of the London Stock Exchange

C Has normal market hours of 08:00 to 17:30

D Is a quote-driven, screen-based electronic market

---

12. A principal trade refers to a trade where

A The firm has priority over the other firms when executing the deal

B The trade is effected on behalf of a customer where the firm's remuneration is by way of commission

C The trade is effected by the firm on its own behalf and for its own account

D The trade is the first undertaken during that day's trading

---

13. Who can perform a gilt repo transaction?

A Any market maker

B Inter-dealer brokers

C Broker-dealers

D Any market participant

---

14. On which of the following services are Global Depository Receipts most likely to be traded?

A International Order Book

B International Bulletin Board

C International Retail Service

D SEATS +

15. Which of the following trading platforms does NOT make use of market makers?

A SETSqx

B ITBB

C IOB

D IRS

16. Shares in which index trade on virt-x?

A S&P 500

B Dax 30

C Hang Seng

D Nikkei

17. Who will an institutional investor contact to buy or sell securities?

A Market Maker

B IDB

C Broker Dealer

D SBLI

18. What is the function of TRAX for Eurobonds?

A Trade reporting service

B Regulator

C Clearing house

D Settlement infrastructure

19. What is the best definition of the repo rate?

A Price at which security is sold in a repo

B Price at which a security can be bought back in a repo

C Percentage difference between sale and repurchase price in a repo

D Percentage difference between cash proceeds and market value of the security in a repo

20. Which of the following is not true of STRIPS?

A All are zero coupon

B Only the Bank of England can strip gilts

C All are registered securities

D Anyone can invest in STRIPS

21. What is the minimum order size for a trade on the IOB?

A 75

B 25

C 50

D 100

22. What is the mandatory quote period for European shares trading on the IRS?

A 08:15 – 16:00

B 09:00 – 15:40

C 09:00 – 15:30

D 08:00 – 16:15

23. A LSE trade executed at 08:00 must be trade reported

A Within three minutes

B Immediately

C By 17:15

D By 22:00 (or earlier dependent on the system)

24. What is the maximum order size on an order driven market?

A Limited to the size of the order book

B Normal Market Size

C 75 × Normal Market Size

D 8 × Normal Market Size

25. Which of the following is true of the uncrossing period in SETS?

A No orders can be input, but deletions and amendments are allowed

B No orders can be deleted or amended, but orders may be input

C No orders can be input, deleted or amended during uncrossing

D No orders can be input or amended, but deletions are allowed

26. What can be inferred from a gilt sale and repurchase agreement?

A Short-term interest rate

B LIBOR

C Repo rate

D Market rate

Answers

1. **D** The London Stock Exchange arranges trades in securities. Index derivative products are traded in the UK on Euronext.liffe

   See Sections 1, 7 and 8 of your Study Book

2. **D** TRAX is a trade confirmation system. Euroclear and Clearstream are Clearing Houses for settlement purposes and also offer depository services. Euroclear and Clearstream communicate through an electronic system known as 'the Bridge'

   See Section 8.4 of your Study Book

3. **B** Only limit orders and market orders can be placed during the opening, closing and intraday call (auction) periods. Therefore, only these two types of order can be matched during the uncrossing period following an auction. Achieving price improvement means that the order may be executed at better than the stated limit price when the order is input

   See Section 3.2 of your Study Book

4. **D** To guarantee best execution, SETS will match incoming sell orders with the top of the buy side on the order book. In this case, the sell order can match through a multiple fill at 855 with orders A and B

   See Section 3.1 of your Study Book

5. **D** Committed Principals are market makers on the International Retail Service who are obliged to display limit orders during the Mandatory Quote Period (MQP)

   See Section 5.3 of your Study Book

6. **D** If a fill or kill order cannot be fully matched, then the whole order will be eliminated from the system. In this case, since we cannot match the full 5,000 shares at a price of 757 or better, it will be eliminated

   See Section 3.2 of your Study Book

7. **C** Most AIM shares will trade on SETSqx. The IOB and the IRS are international platforms and SETS is for the most liquid stocks

   See Section 1.3 of your Study Book

8. **B** A fill or kill order must be either fully filled or totally killed. It cannot be partially filled

   See Section 3.2 of your Study Book

9. **C** TRAX is ICMA's trade and transaction reporting system. It cannot be used to communicate with Euroclear

   See Section 8.4 of your Study Book

10. **B** Best execution in SETS securities must be achieved using the current order book as a benchmark. Since this sell order would be matched at 755 on the buy side of the order book, the price offered must be 755 or better

    See Section 2.5 of your Study Book

11. **A** virt-x is a Recognised Investment Exchange operating an order-driven service known as the 'instant auction'. Like SETS, all trades are published immediately and it operates between 08:00 and 16:30

See Section 6.1 of your Study Book

12. **C** A principal trade is one for the firm's own account. Alternatively, the firm can act as agent when it undertakes a trade on behalf of a customer

See Section 1.2 of your Study Book

13. **D** A repo is a sale and repurchase agreement at an agreed price. Various parties will use them, including those listed in the question

See Section 7.5.2 of your Study Book

14. **A** IOB trades mostly Global Depository Receipts, ITBB trades mostly Asian equities, IRS trades blue chip European and US equities and SEATS + trades less liquid UK-listed and AIM securities

See Section 5.1 of your Study Book

15. **C** The International Order Book (IOB) is purely order driven. The other services mentioned all make use of Market Makers, either quoting prices (in the case of IRS) or entering Committed Principal orders (in the case of the International Bulletin Board and SETSqx)

See Section 5.1 of your Study Book

16. **B** virt-x is an exchange for blue chip European equities, therefore Dax 30 (the German index) is the correct answer. Answers A, C and D are indices for the US, Hong Kong and Japanese markets respectively

See Section 6.1 of your Study Book

17. **C** There would be no reason why an institutional investor could not contact a market maker, but providing execution services to clients (whether institutional or private) is part of the general role of broker dealers, rather than the specific duties of market makers

See Section 1.2 of your Study Book

18. **A** Eurobond trades should be reported in TRAX within 30 minutes of execution. The regulator for the Eurobond market is ICMA (the International Capital Markets Association)

See Section 8.4 of your Study Book

19. **C** The cost of buying back the security in the second leg of a repo is equal to the original cash transferred on sale, plus the cost of interest at the 'repo rate'

See Section 7.5.2 of your Study Book

20. **B** It is gilt-edged market makers (GEMMs) who are permitted to strip certain gilts, not the Bank of England

See Section 7.5.1 of your Study Book

21. **C** The existence of a minimum order size is a feature of the IOB but not of SETS

See Section 5.1 of your Study Book

22. **A** You need to be aware of the key timings in different markets

See Section 5.3 of your Study Book

23. **A** Remember to distinguish between trade reporting and transaction reporting. Answer D would be correct for transaction reporting

See Section 9.2 of your Study Book

24. **A** There are no rules restricting the size of the order, but in practice you will only be able to fully execute an order at a given time if there are enough outstanding orders on the book to fill your trade

See Section 3.2.2 of your Study Book

25. **C** Essentially the system is 'frozen' while uncrossing takes place

See Section 3.3 of your Study Book

26. **C** The repo rate will determine the amount for which the gilts are repurchased in the second leg

See Section 7.5.2 of your Study Book

4. Settlement

Questions

1. **What was introduced to eliminate intraday risk on foreign currency transactions?**

   A CLS

   B LCH. Clearnet

   C CHAPS

   D TARGET

---

2. **Currency trades between the Bank of England and the Japanese Government would take place via which of the following?**

   A CLS

   B BACS

   C DVP

   D CREST

---

3. **Which of the following bodies regulates Euroclear UK and Ireland?**

   A The Financial Services Association

   B The Bank of England

   C The Financial Services Authority

   D The Financial Services and Markets Act

---

4. **All of the following are expenses an investor could expect to pay when buying shares in the UK, except**

   A Withholding tax

   B Stamp duty

   C Stockbroker's commission

   D CREST settlement fees

---

5. **The on-register date for dividends is decided by who in the UK?**

   A The Stock Exchange

   B HM Revenue and Customs

   C The company

   D The FSA

6. All of the following are true of both registered and bearer shares, except

A Both give voting rights to the holder

B Both are transferred by means of a stock transfer form

C Both give the right to participate in dividends

D Both can be listed on the Stock Exchange

---

7. German equities that have traded on a domestic German equity exchange will settle through which of the following institutions?

A CREST

B Euroclear

C Clearstream

D EUREX

---

8. Which of the following is not true of stamp duty?

A Stamp duty is payable by the buyer of shares to be converted into ADRs

B Stamp duty is not payable on the purchase of new issues

C Stamp duty is not payable by charities

D Stamp duty is payable by the vendor of equity securities

---

9. What is the Ad Valorem UK tax on a share purchase for £187.60?

A £1.50

B 50p

C £1.00

D £5.00

---

10. What is the standard settlement period for UK equities?

A Same day

B T + 1

C T + 3

D T + 5

---

11. What is the settlement convention on the NYSE?

A T + 1

B T + 3

C T + 5

D T + 2

12. How long can a share be traded special ex-div prior to the ex-div date in the UK?

A 5 business days

B 10 business days

C 15 business days

D 20 business days

---

13. Which of the following incurs stamp duty on purchase in the UK?

A UK registered share

B UK bearer share

C Call options on UK-registered share

D Foreign shares traded on the LSE

---

14. Which of the following statements best describes the term 'free of payment'?

A The simultaneous transfer of securities and cash in settlement of a trade

B The transfer of free bonus shares to a shareholder entitled to the benefit

C Settlement of a trade which takes place using separate transfers of cash and securities

D The settlement of a transaction by a global custodian, which does not incur separate settlement charges

---

15. All of the following are true of Euroclear UK and Ireland, except

A It provides book entry transfer

B It provides for delivery versus payment

C It is owned and operated by the Bank of England

D It offers facilities for both dematerialised and paper settlement

---

16. Which of the following is true of both Stamp Duty and Stamp Duty Reserve Tax (SDRT) in the UK?

A Both payable within CREST

B Both payable on most paper-based transfers of UK shares

C Both payable on most dematerialised transfers of UK shares

D Both based on ½% of consideration paid

---

17. Which of the following statements is true concerning shares registered into the name of a nominee?

A The company will not know the name of the underlying beneficial owner

B Any benefits offered by a company to its shareholders are lost by the underlying beneficial owner

C Nominees can only be used for certificated holdings

D Once an underlying beneficial owner holds a 5% or more stake in the company that fact must be notified to the company

18. When dealing in UK debenture stock, when would you normally expect to settle the bargain?

A Three business days hence

B Two days hence

C The next day

D On account day

19. Which of the following settles T + 1 in the UK?

A Equities

B New issues

C Global Depositary Receipts

D American Depository Receipts

Answers

1. **A** This is the abbreviation for Continuous Linked Settlement, which came into existence specifically to eliminate intraday currency risk (also known as Herstatt risk).

   See Section 2 of your Study Book

2. **A** As a major international currency trade, this would be settled via CLS

   See Section 2 of your Study Book

3. **C** Euroclear UK and Ireland is regulated by the FSA, the Financial Services Authority, as a Recognised Clearing House

   See Section 1.3.1 of your Study Book

4. **A** Withholding tax applies to dividends. The CREST settlement fees are likely to be incorporated into the stockholder's commission in practice

   See Section 1.6.1 of your Study Book

5. **C** The on-register (books close) date is decided by the company. The date the share starts to trade ex-div is decided by the London Stock Exchange. The on-register date is historically set for a Friday. Given standard settlement of T + 3, the LSE sets the ex-div date two business days prior to the Friday, i.e. on the Wednesday

   See Section 1.4.1 of your Study Book

6. **B** Bearer shares do not need a stock transfer form – physical delivery of the share is sufficient

   See Section 1.6.1 of your Study Book

7. **C** Clearstream was formerly Deutsche Börse Clearing. EUREX Clearing will act as the central counterparty to the trade

   See Section 1.3 of your Study Book

8. **D** Stamp duty is only payable by the purchaser and not the vendor (seller)

   See Section 1.6.1 of your Study Book

9. **D** £5.00 per £1,000 or part thereof (i.e. ½% rounded up to the next £5.00). As there is no answer rounded to the nearest penny, we assume the question is asking for stamp duty, not SDRT

   See Section 1.6.1 of your Study Book

10. **C** Equities settle at T + 3

    See Section 1.3 of your Study Book

11. **B** Standard settlement convention in the US is T + 3

    See Section 1.3 of your Study Book

12. **B** Shares can trade special-ex in the ten business days prior to the ex-dividend period commencing

See Section 1.5 of your Study Book

13. **A** Stamp duty does not apply upon the purchase of the call option, only if the call option is exercised

See Section 1.6.1 of your Study Book

14. **C** Free of payment is also called free delivery. This is when the security transfer and the cash transfer take place at different times

See Section 1.1.1 of your Study Book

15. **C** CREST is owned by CRESTco, who merged with Euroclear in 2002. Although it is mainly used for dematerialised settlement, it can also be used for paper settlement.

See Section 1.3.1 of your Study Book

16. **D** CREST will only deal with SDRT obligations. Certificated transfers would give rise to Stamp Duty, but dematerialised transfers would give rise to SDRT. Both are based on ½% of consideration, but SDRT is rounded to the nearest penny whereas Stamp Duty is rounded up to the next £5

See Section 1.6.1 of your Study Book

17. **A** If shares are registered in the name of a nominee, the company will not know the name of the underlying beneficial owner unless the beneficial owner holds a **3%** stake, in which case the company must be notified. Any benefits offered by a company, e.g. dividends or rights issues, should be offered to the beneficial holder. Nominees are commonly used in CREST for dematerialised (uncertificated) holdings

See Section 1.2.1 of your Study Book

18. **A** Debentures are a type of corporate bond

See Section 1.3.5 of your Study Book

19. **B** Rights issues (and other types of new issue) settle T + 1

See Section 1.3.5 of your Study Book

5. Special Regulatory Requirements – Securities

Questions

1. **When an individual acquires a material interest in a company, the company should be notified of this within**

   A One business day
   B Two business days
   C Three business days
   D Four business days

2. **Control of a company is achieved in legal terms when a shareholder takes their stake in the company to more than**

   A 20%
   B 25%
   C 30%
   D 50%

3. **Under SEC Rule 15a-6, which of the following can a UK firm not do?**

   A Deal on a European market for an American customer, where the business was unsolicited
   B Deal with a US broker
   C Provide research to major US institutional investors, indicating that the firm should be used for business in the stock recommended
   D Visit US institutional investors accompanied by a US registered broker

4. **Which of the following is false in relation to the Panel on Takeovers and Mergers?**

   A Its rulebook sets out the Conduct of Business Rules for regulated activities
   B It is a non-statutory body which derives its powers from the City institutions which make up its members
   C It regulates the takeover of companies
   D A major premise is that all shareholders should be treated fairly in a bid for a company's shares

5. **In the USA, what value would a company need to be in order to be considered a major institutional investor?**

   A $200,000
   B $1.5m
   C $2m
   D $100m

Answers

Please note that references to the Study Book refer to the general section concerning the question subject. The purpose is to enable you to revise the whole subject and may not necessarily explain every fine detail. Should you have any further questions, please contact a BPP Profession Education tutor on 020 7786 5999.

1. **B** This relates to the Disclosure Rules which require disclosures by material and notifiable interest. A material interest is an investor who has a 3% or more holding in the company (aggregated with those investments of connected parties, e.g. spouses, infant children but **not** siblings). Once the investor reaches 3% (10% for notifiable interest) and every time the investor changes the holding by going through a percentage point, e.g. 6.7% to 7.1%, the investor must inform the company by the end of the second business day following the day of trade, i.e. T + 2

   See Section 1.4.2 of your Study Book

2. **D** 30% or more gives **effective** control under the Listing Rules

   See Section 1.1 of your Study Book

3. **C** Rule 15a-6 provides UK firms with the right to provide research to large institutional investors, but not to indicate that they should be used for business as a result

   See Section 3 of your Study Book

4. **A** The Panel on Takeovers and Mergers is one of the few bodies that remains outside of the FSA. The Panel is interested in regulating takeovers, using the 'Blue Book', and ensuring all shareholders are treated fairly in a takeover

   See Section 1.2 of your Study Book

5. **D** This relates to Rule 15A-6 which allows overseas firms to provide research to major institutional investors in the US without registering with the SEC

   See Section 3.2 of your Study Book

6. Accounting Analysis

Questions

1. **If the dividend per share is 10.5p, dividend cover is 1.5x and net dividend yield 7%, what is the P/E ratio?**

   A 11.9×

   B 9.5×

   C 13.2×

   D 8.4×

---

2. **Which of the following payments is not a revenue expense?**

   A Distribution costs

   B Auditor's fee

   C Depreciation on machinery

   D Loan repayment

---

3. **In which of the following categories would prepayments be found in a set of accounts?**

   A Current assets

   B Current liabilities

   C Non-current assets

   D Fixed payables falling due after more than one year

---

4. **A company has dividend cover of 1.25×, a net dividend of 12p and a P/E ratio of 20. What is the net dividend yield?**

   A 5%

   B 4%

   C 5.3%

   D 6.25%

---

5. **If share capital is £100m, the share premium account £70m, retained earnings £125m, turnover £320m and liabilities total £130m, what is the value of all assets, both non-current and current?**

   A £425m

   B £615m

   C £190m

   D £165m

6. **A share has a P/E ratio of 10, EPS of 30p and dividend cover of 2.4×. What is the net dividend yield?**

   A 4.17%

   B 5.21%

   C 5.56%

   D 5.65%

---

7. **What is indicated by a dividend cover figure of less than one?**

   A The company is insolvent

   B The dividend payment has been partly satisfied by accumulated profits

   C The company has exhausted its distributable reserves

   D The company cannot pay a dividend this year

---

8. **If a company issues shares with a nominal value of 25p at a price of 75p each, the excess of the issue price over the nominal value will be put in**

   A Share capital

   B Share premium account reserve

   C Capital surplus reserve

   D Retained earnings

---

9. **All of the following are part of shareholders' funds, except**

   A Authorised share capital

   B Retained earnings

   C Share premium account reserve

   D Capital redemption reserve

---

10. **A retailer originally purchased an item of inventory for £150. The item was then put on sale for £200. Subsequently, due to a change in market conditions, the retailer marked down the item's price to £140 in order to clear the obsolete inventory and it is estimated that a further £5 will be incurred in selling the item. At what value would the inventory be recognised in the balance sheet of the retailer?**

    A £150

    B £200

    C £135

    D £140

---

11. **Which of the following is true of the retained earnings shown on the balance sheet?**

    A It represents the profits generated for the financial year

    B It is a distributable reserve and can be used to cover payment of dividends to shareholders

    C It cannot be used to finance a bonus issue

    D It can never show a negative balance, as the company would then be insolvent

12. A company has an earnings yield of 6.42%, a net dividend per share of 2.7p and a current market price per share of 140p. What is its dividend cover?

A 3.75×

B 3.00×

C 3.33×

D 4.69×

---

13. Which of the following would not be depreciated?

A Freehold buildings

B Freehold land

C Trademarks

D Plant and machinery

---

14. All of the following would normally be included in current liabilities, except

A Trade accounts payable

B Corporation tax paid

C Accruals

D Overdrafts

---

15. Which of the following is not a current asset?

A Prepayments

B Inventory

C Cash

D Goodwill on consolidation

---

16. Which of the following would not be an intangible non-current asset in the balance sheet?

A Purchased goodwill

B Trademarks

C Investments

D Capitalised research and development costs

---

17. All of the following would be found in the income statement, except

A Taxation

B Interest payable

C Prepayments

D Costs of sales

18. Reserves in a company's accounts are part of

A Shareholders' funds

B Assets

C Profits

D Liabilities

---

19. Accruals would be found in which of the following categories in a company's accounts?

A Current liabilities

B Current assets

C Other income

D Cash

---

20. All of the following are categories of non-current assets, except

A Investments

B Intangible

C Tangible

D Inventory

---

21. Bank overdrafts would appear in which of the following balance sheet categories?

A Cash

B Current liabilities

C Non-current liabilities

D Provisions

---

22. Which of the following appear in the income statement for the year?

A Cash

B Accruals and deferred income

C Debentures

D Cost of sales

---

23. A company has operating profits of £300,000 and interest payable of £25,000. Its shareholders' funds are £1,000,000 and long-term loans are £100,000. What is its return on capital employed, where capital employed is defined as non-current assets plus working capital?

A 30.0%

B 27.5%

C 27.3%

D 25.0%

24. Bank plc has an earnings per share figure from its latest accounts of 15p per share. If they declared a dividend of 5p per share, what would be the dividend cover?

A Nil

B A third

C One

D Three

25. ABC's share price is currently standing at £6.50. The EPS has been determined by your company's analyst to be 60p. What is the P/E ratio of ABC?

A 60×

B 11×

C 9×

D 9%

26. A stock pays a dividend of 20p and its current market price is 250p. What is its dividend yield?

A 8%

B 8.88%

C 12.31%

D 14.03%

27. A company issues debentures with a two-year maturity for cash in order to raise further finance for expansion. In the company's balance sheet, this would have the effect of

A Increasing current assets, increasing non-current liabilities

B Increasing current assets, increasing capital

C Increasing non-current liabilities

D Increasing current assets, increasing current liabilities

28. Turnover in a company's income statement represents

A The total value of cash receipts in respect of sales during the period, from both cash and credit sales

B The total value of cash sales during the period

C Total sales less the cost of the goods sold during the period

D The total value of goods sold to customers during the accounting period, whether paid for in cash or not

29. Which of the following relationships is true?

A Price-to-earnings ratio multiplied by earnings per share equals price per share

B Price-to-earnings ratio divided by earnings per share equals price per share

C Price per share multiplied by price-to-earnings ratio equals earnings per share

D Price per share multiplied by earnings per share equals price-to-earnings ratio

30. If A plc has a P/E ratio of 30 and B plc has a P/E ratio of 10, what can we tell about the two companies?

I The market believes that A plc has better future prospects than B plc

II The market believes that B plc has better future prospects than A plc

III The absolute share price of A plc must be higher than B plc

IV We cannot tell from the information given whether A or B's share price is higher in absolute terms

A I and III

B II and III

C I and IV

D II and IV

31. Which of the following would you see on a balance sheet?

A Dividends received

B Net profit

C Intangible assets

D Interest paid

32. Which is generally a property of ratios?

A Forward looking

B Difficult to calculate

C Used for comparison between companies

D Information is difficult to find

33. What is the formula for dividend cover?

A EPS/Gross DPS

B Net DPS/EPS

C EPS/Net DPS

D Gross DPS/EPS

34. What is revenue, less direct and indirect costs?

A Net income

B Retained earnings

C Operating profit

D Gross profit

35. How will a company's balance sheet be affected by a capitalisation issue?

A Share premium account will increase

B Reserves will decrease

C Reserves will increase

D Share capital will decrease

36. What would be likely P/E and dividend yield values for a high growth company?

A High P/E, low dividend yield

B Low P/E, low dividend yield

C High P/E, high dividend yield

D Low P/E, high dividend yield

Answers

1. **B** $\frac{\text{EPS}}{\text{DPS}}$ = Dividend cover

Hence

EPS = Dividend cover × DPS = 1.5× × 10.5p = 15.75p

$\frac{\text{Dividend}}{\text{Price}}$ = Net dividend yield

Hence

$\frac{\text{Dividend}}{\text{Net dividend yield}}$ = price

$\frac{10.5\text{p}}{0.07}$ = 150p = price

$\frac{P}{E} = \frac{\text{Price}}{\text{EPS}} = \frac{150\text{p}}{15.75\text{p}} = 9.5\times$

See Section 5.5.2 of your Study Book

2. **D** This would be a repayment of capital and will not go through the income statement

See Section 3.3.2 of your Study Book

3. **A** The company owns an asset which will be received shortly

See Section 2.5 of your Study Book

4. **B** Net div 12p

Dividend cover 1.25×, therefore

EPS = 12p × 1.25× = 15p

P/E = 20   EPS = 15p

Market price = P/E × EPS

= 20 × 15p = 300p

Net dividend yield = $\frac{12\text{p}}{300\text{p}} \times 100 = 4\%$

See Section 5.5.3 of your Study Book

5. **A** Assets – Liabilities = Shareholders' funds

∴ Shareholders' funds + Liabilities = Assets

£100m + £70m + £125m + £130m = £425m

See Section 2.2 of your Study Book

6. **A** EPS = 30p, P/E = 10

Therefore

Price = P/E × EPS

= 10 × 30p = £3

EPS = 30p

$$\text{Dividend cover} = 2.4\times = \frac{\text{EPS}}{\text{DPS}}$$

Therefore

$$\text{Net dividend} = \frac{\text{EPS}}{\text{Dividend cover}}$$

$$= \frac{30p}{2.4\times} = 12.5p$$

$$\frac{12.5p}{£3} \times 100 = 4.17\%$$

See Section 5.5 of your Study Book

7. **B** This is an uncovered dividend as the company has decided to pay a dividend which is greater than this year's profits.

See Section 5.5.4 of your Study Book

8. **B** The share capital account relates to the nominal value of issued shares. The retained earnings (on the balance sheet) records the accumulated profit/losses since trading began which have not already been paid out as a dividend or transferred to other reserves. The capital surplus reserves is a made-up term!

See Section 2.12 of your Study Book

9. **A** It is called-up share capital that appears in shareholders' funds, not authorised share capital. Authorised share capital is determined when a company is initially set up and is found in the Memorandum of Association

See Section 2.11 of your Study Book

10. **C**

		£
Lower of	– cost	150
	– net realisable value (140 – 5)	135

See Section 2.5 of your Study Book

11. **B** It can be negative. A company is only insolvent if it cannot pay its debts as they fall due. Bonus issues can be accounted for by a transfer from most reserves

See Section 2.15 of your Study Book

12. **C** Dividend cover = $\frac{\text{Earnings yield}}{\text{Dividend yield}} = \frac{6.42\%}{\text{Dividend yield}}$

$$\text{Dividend yield} = \frac{\text{Net dividend}}{\text{Price}} \times 100$$

$$= \frac{2.7p}{140p} \times 100 = 1.93\%$$

$$\therefore \text{Dividend cover} = \frac{6.42\%}{1.93\%} = 3.33\times$$

See Section 5.5.4 of your Study Book

13. **B** Although trademarks would technically be amortised, B is the best answer

See Section 2.4 of your Study Book

14. **B** Corporation tax paid would be shown in the company's cash flow statement

See Section 2.6 of your Study Book

15. **D** Goodwill is an intangible fixed asset. Inventory refers to inventories of goods held by the company for resale

See Section 2.5 of your Study Book

16. **C** Investments have their own section in non-current assets

See Section 2.4 of your Study Book

17. **C** Prepayments are found in current assets on the balance sheet. These represent items which have been paid for, but the full benefit has not been received

See Section 2.5 of your Study Book

18. **A** Representing any source of funds not due to called-up share capital

See Section 2.2.4 of your Study Book

19. **A** For example, a firm that has used electricity over a period, but has not yet received the bill

See Section 2.7.1 of your Study Book

20. **D** Inventory would be part of current assets

See Section 2.4 of your Study Book

21. **B** As the money is repayable on demand it is a current liability

See Section 2.6 of your Study Book

22. **D** Cash is a current asset; accruals and deferred income are current liabilities, while debentures are non-current liabilities

See Section 3.2.1 of your Study Book

23. **C** Capital employed = Non-current assets + Working capital

= Non-current assets + Current assets – Current liabilities

= Shareholders' funds + Long-term liabilities

= £1m + £0.1m

= £1.1m

$$\text{Return on capital employed} = \frac{\text{Operating profit (EBIT)}}{\text{Capital employed}}$$

$$= \frac{£0.3\text{m}}{£1.1\text{m}} \times 100 = 27.3\%$$

Note that the interest payable figure is a 'red herring' (distractor)

See Section 5.2.1 of your Study Book

24. **D** 15p divided by 5p is 3, i.e. earnings cover the dividend three times

See Section 5.5.4 of your Study Book

25. **B** $\text{P/E} = \frac{\text{Price}}{\text{Earnings}} = \frac{650\text{p}}{60\text{p}} = 10.83\times$

Therefore, 11 is the nearest available answer. Note that P/E ratios are normally presented as a multiple rather than as a percentage

See Section 5.5.2 of your Study Book

26. **A** The net dividend yield is the actual dividend paid expressed as a percentage of the share price. In this case

(20p/250p) × 100 = 8%

See Section 5.5.3 of your Study Book

27. **A** The debentures are a liability. Since they have a two-year maturity, they will be shown under non-current liabilities. The cash will be part of current assets

See Section 2.2 of your Study Book

28. **D** Turnover is the total value of goods sold, whether they are paid for using cash or credit. If costs of goods sold is deducted from this figure, gross profit is calculated

See Section 3.2.1 of your Study Book

29. **A** $\text{P/E ratio} = \frac{\text{Price per share}}{\text{Earnings per shares}}$

Hence

P/E ratio × Earnings per share = Price per share

See Section 5.5.2 of your Study Book

30. **C** If A plc has a higher P/E ratio, it means that the market believes that A plc has better prospects than B plc, presuming that the two companies are from the same sector. There is no way of knowing what the actual share prices are without knowing what the earnings of the two companies are

See Section 5.5.2 of your Study Book

31. **C** The other items would be found in the income statement

See Section 3.2.1 of your Study Book

32. **C** Although it is possible to use forecast information to calculate forward-looking ratios, and certain ratios can involve complex calculations based on obscure information, none of these applies to the ratios you need to learn about for the exam. However, ratios can in general be used to compare companies

See Section 5.1.4 of your Study Book

33. **C** It is specifically the net dividend per share number that should be used (i.e. the amount the investor receives after 10% withholding tax). Although this may seem inconsistent, the net amount is all the company actually pays out. The 10% tax is 'deemed' by the HM Revenue & Customs to have been paid already, as the company itself has already paid corporation tax on its profits

See Section 5.5.4 of your Study Book

34. **C** Gross profit takes account of direct costs (i.e. cost of sales) only, whereas operating profit takes account of indirect costs as well (e.g. administration and distribution costs)

See Section 3.2.1 of your Study Book

35. **B** The bonus or capitalisation issue increases the share capital of the company, as a greater nominal value of shares will be in issue. But as the total shareholders funds stays the same, if share capital increases then the reserves must decrease by the same amount. The specific reserve which is reduced in this instance is the share premium account

See Section 2.12 of your Study Book

36. **A** The perception of growth would make the company's shares relatively expensive compared to current earnings and divided levels

See Sections 5.5.2 and 5.5.3 of your Study Book

7. Risk and Reward

1. **A security that preserves the value of its purchasing power over time, despite increases in the general price level, is known as**

   A A risk-free asset

   B An indentured security

   C An inflation hedge

   D A negative correlation inflation stock

2. **Compared to general insurance business, life assurance related business generally dictates that the insurance company holds more**

   A Longer term assets

   B Treasury bills

   C Commercial paper

   D Certificates of deposit

3. **Rank the following investments in order of risk, with the riskiest first**

   I Traded options

   II Equity shares in quoted companies

   III Convertible debt in quoted companies

   IV Gilts

   A I, II, III, IV

   B I, III, II, IV

   C II, I, III, IV

   D III, II, I, IV

4. **In order to achieve a high return/high risk profile, you would invest in**

   A A UK stock market tracker fund

   B A US fixed income fund

   C A Japanese fixed income fund

   D A South American equity fund

5. **The assets required by a mature pension fund are**

   A Long-term, high risk

   B Short-term, high risk

   C Long-term, low risk

   D Short-term, low risk

6. Which of the following gilts would a higher rate taxpayer find most suitable to invest in if he expected interest rates to fall?

A High coupon short-dated

B Low coupon short-dated

C High coupon long-dated

D Low coupon long-dated

---

7. What is the best investment for a UK higher rate tax payer with a very low risk profile?

A Short term, high coupon bonds

B Convertible bonds

C Medium term, medium coupon bonds

D Medium term, low coupon bonds

---

8. Which would have short-term, low return investments?

A Life assurance fund

B Pension fund

C General insurance company

D Investment trust

---

9. Which of the following investments is least volatile?

A A building society deposit

B A Treasury bill

C A medium dated gilt

D A corporate bond

Answers

1. **C** As the asset will rise in line with the general rise in prices, it will provide a hedge against inflation

   See Section 5.2 of your Study Book

2. **A** Life assurance will have longer term liabilities to pay bonuses at the end of 20 or so years. Therefore, it is best to match these with longer term asset holdings

   See Section 4.1.2 of your Study Book

3. **A** Gilts are less risky than company debt, as they are backed by the UK Government

   See Section 1.2 of your Study Book

4. **D** Equities are more risky than fixed income, and South American equities are more risky than US equities

   See Section 1.2 of your Study Book

5. **D** Mature funds are for people close to retirement, hence short-term and low risk

   See Section 4.1.1 of your Study Book

6. **D** This will be the most volatile bond, as it has the highest duration and, consequently, will provide the greatest capital gain. In addition, the low coupon will minimise the tax payment

   See Section 2.1.1 of your Study Book

7. **A** In fact, the ideal investment would be short term, low coupon bonds. However, as this option is not available, we have to choose between the bond with the lowest risk (a short-dated, high coupon bond, as this will be the least volatile) or the bond with the optimum tax impact (which will be the low coupon bond). As the investor is said to have a VERY low risk profile, this points us towards the low risk choice

   See Section 2.1.1 of your Study Book

8. **C** Life assurance and pension funds will generally have longer term objectives and in theory should choose investments to match these objectives. Investment Trusts' investment strategies will vary depending upon the objectives laid down in the company's constitutional documents. General insurance funds have potential liabilities in the short term, and therefore tend to invest in short term, low risk investments

   See Section 4.1.3 of your Study Book

9. **A** The values of the others will all be to some extent affected by changes in interest rate, but the value of cash held on deposit will stay the same

   See Section 2.2.1 of your Study Book

Practice Examinations

Contents

Candidates for the **Unit 4 (Securities and Financial Derivatives)** exam should use these Practice Examinations in conjunction with those in the separate Financial Derivatives Question Bank.

This will replicate the structure of the exam, which contains 100 questions on Securities, followed by 70 questions on Financial Derivatives (in addition to a small number of 'trial' questions which do not count towards your final mark).

Practice Examination 1

100 Questions in 2 Hours

1. **What is the best definition of the REPO rate?**

   A Price at which security is sold in a REPO

   B Price at which a security can be bought back in a REPO

   C Percentage difference between sale and repurchase price in a REPO

   D Percentage difference between cash proceeds and market value of the security in a REPO

2. **When does the opening auction start on the IOB?**

   A 08:00

   B 08:50

   C 07:50

   D 07:15

3. **Which is the best measure of an investor's return on equity?**

   A Dividend yield

   B Earnings yield

   C Company profits

   D Net income

4. **Gilts which are classified as shorts by the Debt Management Office have what maximum period to run to maturity?**

   A One year

   B Five years

   C Seven years

   D Ten years

5. **Which of the following issues is most likely to give the fairest treatment for existing shareholders of a company?**

   A Selective marketing

   B Offer for sale

   C Open offer

   D Rights issue

6. **The current spot rate £/$ is $2.0375-$2.0385 which means £1 is worth $2.0375 or $2.0385. The forward quote is at a current premium for dollars of 50 pips. Which of the following is the correct forward rate?**

A $2.0425-$2.0435

B $2.0325-$2.0335

C $2.0875-$2.0885

D $1.9875-$1.9885

7. **All of the following are true of warrants, except**

A They have the right to subscribe for new shares

B They can have intrinsic value

C They can have time value

D They form part of share capital

8. **Which of the following investments would be most suitable for a person nearing retirement with inadequate pension prospects?**

A Traded options

B High growth equity shares

C Penny shares

D High yielding gilts

9. **Under the City Code, acquiring shares that take a total holding over which percentage level would lead to a mandatory offer?**

A 20%

B 30%

C 50%

D 90%

10. **When does a spot trade for US dollars settle?**

A T + 2

B T + 3

C T + 4

D T + 5

11. **A company's shares are trading at 180p. If its latest earnings were 9p per share, which of the following is the P/E ratio?**

A 0.05×

B 5×

C 20×

D 2×

12. The price-earnings (P/E) ratio is given by

A Current share price divided by latest total earnings

B Current share price divided by average total earnings over the past three years

C Current share price divided by average earnings per share over the last three years

D Current share price divided by earnings per share declared for the last financial year

13. What are the trading hours on virt-x?

A 07:15-17:15

B 08:30-16:00

C 08:00-16:30

D 07:30-16:45

14. Which of the following is the best definition of a reverse repo?

A The purchase and resale of an asset on an agreed date

B The sale of an asset followed by a repurchase at an agreed date

C The sale and repurchase of an asset

D The purchase and resale of an asset at an agreed price

15. Eurobonds usually pay coupons

A Annually

B Six-monthly

C Quarterly

D Monthly

16. Which of the following is NOT traded on IOB?

A ADRs

B Traditional options

C GDRs

D Hong Kong securities

17. The SETS order book for a particular security is as represented below. Your client wants to sell 5,000 of the shares at 159 worst price. If you place the order on SETS, which of the statements below is true?

	Buy			Sell			
	Time	Volume	Price	Price	Volume	Time	
A	09:41	1,700	157	159	3,500	08:55	D
B	09:58	2,300	157	159	1,000	09:15	E
C	09:57	1,400	157	160	2,300	10:25	F

A The order will be matched in full through a multiple fill

B The order will be placed above order D at the top of the sell side of the order book awaiting matching orders

C The order will be matched with buy orders A, B and part of C and the unexecuted balance of order C will be eliminated

D The order will be placed above order F on the sell side of the order book

18. What best describes securities that trade on SETS?

A FTSE 100 shares only

B FTSE 100 + reserve securities + securities underlying options traded on Euronext.Liffe

C FTSE 100 + securities underlying options traded on Euronext.Liffe

D FTSE 250 shares

19. A shareholder who owns 17½% of the shares of ABC plc, a listed company, sells part of his shareholding leaving a holding after the sale of 16½%. What disclosure obligations does the shareholder have?

A Disclose the sale to the company concerned within two business days

B Disclose the sale to the company concerned by noon the next day

C Disclose the sale to the market within two business days

D Disclose the sale to the market by noon the next day

20. How many months can ADR's be traded in pre-release form?

A 1 month

B 3 months

C 6 months

D 12 months

21. Which two of the following constitute best execution under SETS?

I The highest bid price on the order book

II The lowest bid price on the order book

III The highest offer price on the order book

IV The lowest offer price on the order book

A I and III

B II and IV

C II and III

D I and IV

22. Which one of the following is not true of NOMADs?

A They guide a firm through the AIM process

B They are kept on to advise the directors on their continuing responsibilities

C They help to trade the shares

D They must be approved by the LSE

23. Under SEC Rule 15A-6, which of the following can a UK firm not do?

A Deal on a European market for an American customer where the business was unsolicited

B Deal with a US broker

C Provide research to major US institutional investors, indicating that the firm should be used for business in the stock recommended

D Visit US institutional investors accompanied by a US registered broker

24. Which of the following is usually true for a general insurance company compared to a life assurance company?

A It will have assets with shorter maturities

B It will invest more in equities

C Its investments will be more illiquid

D Its liabilities will be longer dated

25. If share prices fall, the effect on a convertible bond price is

A Up

B Down

C No change, as both move independently

D Indeterminate

26. You hold £10,000 of a 10% two-year bond (annual coupon). The yield is 8%. What is the price today?

A £9,499.31

B £10,430.73

C £10,356.65

D £11,185.19

27. A company has a 4% non-cumulative preference share in issue. In 2005 and 2006, no dividends are paid; in 2007, 3p is paid to each ordinary share. How much would be recorded by way of dividend by the holders of the preference shares in 2007?

A 7p

B 12%

C 4%

D Nil

28. Based on the information below, which of the following statements is true?

The SETS order book for a particular security is as follows.

Buy			Sell		
Time	Volume	Price	Price	Volume	Time
08:41	1,500	459.00	460.00	5,500	08:55
09:58	2,560	459.00	460.00	1,000	09:15
09:57	800	458.75	460.50	800	10:25

A broker-dealer places an at best buy order on SETS for 10,000 of these shares.

A The order will be matched with all existing sell orders and the unexecuted balance of 2,700 shares carried forward on the order book

B The order will be matched with all existing sell orders and the remainder rejected

C The order will be matched with all existing buy orders and the unexecuted balance of 5,140 shares carried forward on the order book

D The order will be matched with all existing buy orders and the remainder rejected

29. A certificated equity trade takes place on Tuesday 13 June. The share's books close date is Friday 16 June. The trade settles on Thursday 22 June. Which is true?

A The seller is entitled to the dividend since settlement did not occur until after the book's close date

B The dividend will be shared between the buyer and the seller on a pro rata basis

C The buyer's broker will be able to claim the dividend from the seller's broker

D The buyer's broker will have to pay the dividend to compensate the buyer for the late settlement

30. Which of the following does not require marketing?

A Offer for sale

B Offer for subscription

C Placing

D Introduction

---

31. Which of the following is not required in a set of published company accounts?

A Balance sheet

B Income statement

C Cash flow statement

D Profit forecast

---

32. All of the following are means of effecting an offer for sale, except

A Fixed price offer

B Bookbuilding

C Tender offer

D Rights issue

---

33. The mandatory quote period for most European equities on the International Retail Service is

A 08:15 to 16:00

B 08:00 to 16:30

C 08:00 to 16:15

D 09:00 to 15:30

---

34. Which two of the following transactions need to be reported to the company?

I Acquisition of 6% of a public limited company

II Acquisition of 10% of a private company

III Acquisition of 0.8% to an existing holding of 7.2% of a private company

IV Disposal of 0.6% from an existing holding of 8.0% of a public limited company

A III and IV

B II and III

C I and IV

D I and III

---

35. Which bonds offer different tranches and risks?

A Corporate debt

B Senior debt

C CDOs

D Debentures

36. Which of the following is not an option open to an investor when an issuer has announced an equity rights issue?

A To trade the nil paid rights

B Partial acceptance of rights

C Blocking the issue of their share allotment

D Accepting the rights and buying the shares in cash

37. A participating preference share has

A Voting rights

B Additional dividend in good year

C Right of conversion to ordinary share

D A role in the management of the company

38. Shares cannot be entered or deleted from the order book in which two of the following situations?

I During a fast market

II During the running of the uncrossing algorithm

III If the share price moves 5%

IV During a suspension in the shares

A I and IV

B III and IV

C II and III

D II and IV

39. The London Stock Exchange trading day runs

A From 00:01 hours to 24:00 hours

B From 08:00 hours to 16:30 hours

C From 09:00 hours to 17:15 hours

D From 07:15 hours to 17:15 hours

40. All of the following could be valid reasons why permission for an introduction to the London Stock Exchange could be granted, except

A The shares are already listed on an overseas exchange

B The shares are the result of a merger between the two listed companies

C The shares are widely held by UK investors

D To gain access to an offshore market to enable stock options to be granted

41. When is Treasury 6¾% 2006-2008 repayable?

A 2006

B At a time selected by the Debt Management Office between 2006 and 2008

C 2008

D The first occasion between 2006 and 2008 when base rate is below the coupon rate

---

42. What is the aim of the virt-x exchange?

A To provide the opportunity for cross-border trading at the equivalence of domestic cost

B To provide real-time price information on all shares listed in the 12 countries making up the Eurozone

C To facilitate trading in smaller listed companies from throughout Europe

D To allow smaller UK companies a facility for trading their shares with reduced compliance responsibilities

---

43. A seller sells a bond a few days before the ex-div date and receives a dividend. Who does the payment of the of the dividend belong to?

A Seller

B Purchaser

C Broker

D Issuer

---

44. What is the lowest NMS band on the LSE?

A 250 shares

B 100 shares

C 500 shares

D 1,000 shares

---

45. A company with six million shares in issue makes a profit of £1.8 million. Given that the current share price is 360p, calculate the P/E.

A 24

B 12

C 15

D 30

---

46. Which of the following gilts pay interest quarterly?

A 2½% Consols

B 3½% War Loan

C 3½% Conversion

D 4% Consols

47. Which two of the following are examples of a centralised depository?

I Euroclear
II London Stock Exchange
III FSA
IV Clearstream

A I and II
B II and III
C I and IV
D III and IV

48. The spot rate for cable is $2.0785 – $2.0803. Given that the forward rate is 0.45c-0.48c dis, at what forward rate will the bank buy US dollars?

A $2.0830
B $2.0851
C $2.0740
D $2.0755

49. Which of the following is false?

A Capital expenditure is expenditure incurred in day-to-day administrative expenses, e.g. electricity, telephone
B Capital expenditure is expenditure on acquiring or enhancing non-current assets or their operating capacity
C Capital expenditure is capitalised on the balance sheet and will subsequently be depreciated through the income statement
D Revenue expenditure is expenditure incurred in acquiring assets to be sold for conversion into cash, e.g. stock

50. When is the earliest day before a gilt is marked ex that it can be dealt special-ex?

A Ten business days
B 14 business days
C 21 calendar days
D Gilts cannot be traded special-ex

51. Which of the following would be a correct definition of a 'sophisticated investor' in the US?

A Net assets of $1m
B Net assets of $2m
C Net assets of $5m
D Net assets of $10m

52. UK Takeover Panel rules apply to

A Listed companies only

B All public companies

C Listed companies with a market capitalisation greater than £5m

D All public companies with a market capitalisation greater than £5m

53. A committed principal on the ITBB is NOT obligated to do which one of the following?

A Quote committed principal orders of at least the normal market size

B Quote firm prices during the MQP

C Enter committed principal orders within 60 seconds of the end of the opening auction period

D Offer to buy or sell to another member firm at its displayed price

54. Which of the following is true about virt-x?

A Publishes trades instantly on the virt-x system

B Is the responsibility of the London Stock Exchange

C Has normal market hours of 08:00 to 17:30

D Is a quote-driven, screen-based electronic market

55. If you buy a share and it is suspended before the settlement date, what should you do?

A Sell the share immediately

B Pay for the share and await a further announcement

C Delay payment until the suspension is lifted

D The trade will be cancelled

56. With regard to reducing foreign exchange risk, the Bank of England pays money into

A CLS

B CHAPS

C CREST

D CHAPSI

57. Which of the following does NOT play a role in the CCP system?

A CREST

B LCH

C LSE

D Clearstream

58. If a warrant on its expiry date has the right to subscribe for a share at a price of £3.00 and the share price is £5.00

A The warrant has a time value of £5.00

B The warrant has a time value of £3.00

C The warrant has a time value of £2.00

D The warrant has no time value

59. If the spot rate for cable is $1.9770-$1.9860 and the forward rate is 0.36-0.35c pm, at what forward rate will the bank sell US dollars?

A $1.9895

B $1.9825

C $1.9736

D $1.9734

60. Place the following investment transactions in order of risk (riskiest first).

I Purchase of future

II Purchase of option

III Purchase of blue chip shares

IV Purchase of small high technology company shares

A IV, I, II, III

B III, IV, II, I

C I, II, IV, III

D I, II, III, IV

61. Into how many securities can a 5-year gilt be stripped?

A Two

B Six

C Ten

D Eleven

62. What is the order of trade matching on virt-x?

A Price, then time

B Time, then price

C Price, then size

D Size, then time

63. A trade in a SETSqx equity dealt at 17:14 and reported at 07:45 the next business day

A Meets the deadlines set for reporting trades to the Stock Exchange

B Will not be published immediately if it is three times the NMS

C Will be identified when published by the D marker

D May result in disciplinary action being taken against the reporting party

64. The quoted bond price is £98 with accrued interest of £2.50. How much does the buyer pay cum div?

A £100.00

B £102.50

C £98.00

D £100.50

65. Which of the following is the correct order in a liquidation?

A Preference shares, deferred shares, ordinary shares, warrants

B Warrants, preference shares, ordinary shares, deferred shares

C Deferred shares, preference shares, ordinary shares, warrants

D Preference shares, ordinary shares, deferred shares, warrants

66. Which of the following can be used to pay a dividend?

A Retained earnings

B Capital redemption reserve

C Revaluation reserve

D Share premium

67. Commercial Paper

A Is an unsecured, interest paying security

B Is an unsecured, non-interest paying security

C Is a secured, interest paying security

D Is a secured, non-interest paying security

68. Which of the following is the correct order of increasing maturity?

A Bills, Bonds, Notes

B Bills, Notes, Bonds

C Notes, Bills, Bonds

D Notes, Bonds, Bills

69. The date that a share starts to trade ex-div is decided by

A The Stock Exchange

B HMRC

C The company

D The FSA

70. Which of the following is true of ADRs?

A They are freely transferable

B They are transferable if registered in good name

C They are registered instruments

D They can only be transferred via the issuing bank

71. An IOB trade of more than eight times NMS conducted away from the order book must be reported

A Within three minutes

B Immediately

C Within two hours

D By market open the following trading day

72. If a company has shareholders' funds of £10m, non-current assets of £2m and non-current liabilities of £5m, what is the total value of its capital employed?

A £15m

B £10m

C £12m

D £5m

73. If a transaction takes place on the international equity market, which settlement conventions will apply?

A The LSE settlement conventions

B The settlement convention of the domestic market in which the equity is listed

C Either the LSE convention or the domestic market convention

D The buyer and seller will agree between themselves

74. Regarding SETS, which of the following is not a type of order?

A Fixed price order

B At best order

C Fill or kill order

D Execute and eliminate

75. Which of the following is not true of an index-linked gilt?

A There is a fixed benefit at the end

B They pay a low coupon

C They are issued with a range of maturities

D The coupon varies with inflation

76. When a gilt is stripped, which of these statements is TRUE?

A The income streams are treated as separate securities

B Each 'strip' pays a separate regulat coupon as well as an amount on redemption

C Only GEMMs can trade the securities once stripped

D The average value of the components is less than the original gilt

77. Which of the following is true with respect to shares?

A Cumulative preference shares often give voting rights if the company has failed to pay a dividend for three years

B ADRs do not carry voting rights

C 'A' class ordinary shares have enhanced voting rights

D Zero coupon preference shares often carry voting rights

78. An investor purchases £10,000 nominal value of a gilts 5.375% 14 May 2018 to settle on 27 June. How many days of accrued interest are in the price and how much is in the accrued interest using an actual/actual conversion?

A 44; £65

B 45; £66

C 44; £66

D 45; £67

79. What is the main purpose of the syndicate in the issuance of Eurobonds?

A To underwrite the issue

B To ensure that the issue is fully taken up

C To support trading in the secondary market

D To ensure regulatory obligations are met

80. All of the following would be permissible limit order prices for a SETS security that is currently trading around 250p, except

A 276.75p

B 254.30p

C 238.00p

D 250.00p

81. **A company issues 10,000 shares with a nominal value of 50p for 80p each. What is the effect on reserves?**

A £5,000

B £8,000

C £3,000

D No effect

82. **Which of the following groups would not be presumed to act in concert according to the Takeover Code?**

A A company and its directors

B A company and the wives of its directors

C A company and its pension fund (which itself is established as a separate entity, legally ringfenced from the company)

D A company and its employees

83. **What is TRUE about warrants?**

A They form part of the issued share capital

B The holder is entitled to vote

C They are a low-risk method of investing in equities

D If exercised new shares will be created

84. **A Section 793 investigation entitles a company to find out whether a person has had an interest in the company**

A In the last three years

B In the last two years

C At any time

D In the last year

85. **Which of the following is not true of warrants?**

A They have time value that decays as they approach expiry

B They form part of the equity share capital of the company

C They have intrinsic value which varies according to the price of the underlying share

D They give a right, not an obligation, to acquire shares

86. **Which of the following is the maximum time period in which a member firm may enter an order in the SETS order book?**

A 00:01 to 24:00

B 07:15 to 17:15

C 07:50 to end of the closing auction

D 08:00 to 16:30

87. **What is the lowest price that must be paid by a firm on entering into a mandatory bid under POTAM rules?**

A Lowest price paid over the last 12 months

B Highest price paid over the last 3 months

C Highest price paid over the last 12 months

D Lowest price paid over the last 3 months

88. **A principal trade refers to a trade where**

A The firm has priority over other firms when executing the deal

B The trade is effected on behalf of a customer where the firm's remuneration is by way of commission

C The trade is effected by the firm on its own behalf and for its own account

D The trade is the first undertaken during that day's trading

89. **Which of the following is true of Committed Principal orders on the International Bulletin Board?**

A They must be replenished to Normal Market Size within one minute of being filled or deleted

B There is no requirement for orders to be maintained in the opening or closing auction periods

C They can only be matched against limit orders from other members

D They must be entered within one minute of the end of the opening auction

90. **The periods for trading gilts special ex and special cum respectively are usually**

A 21 business days before ex-interest date and seven business days before payment date

B 21 calendar days before ex-interest date and seven business days before payment date

C Gilts cannot be traded special ex and seven business days before payment date

D Gilts cannot be traded special ex and seven calendar days before payment date

91. **Dividend cover is calculated by dividing earnings by**

A Net dividend

B Gross dividend

C Dividend yield

D Market price

92. **Which of the following statements is false regarding an Ordinary share?**

A Their holders are entitled to nominal value in the event of liquidation of the company

B Profits after payment of debenture interest, tax and preference share dividends are available for distribution to Ordinary shareholders

C They carry rights to vote at the company's Annual General Meeting

D The rights of Ordinary shareholders, as regards both dividends and repayment of capital, rank below those of unsecured loan stock holders

93. Which of the following is true of the listing requirements for AIM?

A The company must have a nominated adviser

B The company must have a three-year history

C 25% of the shares must be available to the public

D The company must float at least 10% of its shares

94. Which of the following bonds would be the most responsive to a shift of 1% in yields?

A Low-coupon, short-dated

B Low-coupon, long-dated

C High-coupon, short-dated

D High-coupon, long-dated

95. The definition of a warrant is

A Right to subscribe for new shares

B The interest rate on a Eurobond

C An option that is traded

D A share in a split capital investment trust

96. A group acting in concert to buy shares in a target company must disclose their total holding when it reaches or exceeds

A 3%

B 5%

C 10%

D 29.9%

97. A company increases its free float from 80% of the issued share capital to 100%. Assuming that the market price stays the same, what will be the increase in the market capitalisation?

A Nil

B 20%

C 25%

D 40%

98. All of the following usually have voting rights, except

A Preference shares in arrears of five years

B Scrip issue shares

C Ordinary shares

D Debentures

99. If a company has earnings per share of 50p and pays a dividend of 25p, what is the dividend cover?

A 2×

B 0.5×

C 1.6×

D 0.625×

100. Which of these securities are usually registered?

A Equities

B Eurobonds

C Treasury bills

D French Government Bonds

Answers

Please note that references to the Study Book refer to the general section concerning the question subject. The purpose is to enable you to revise the whole subject and may not necessarily explain every fine detail. Should you have any further questions, please contact a BPP Professional Education tutor on 020 7786 5900.

1. **C** The cost of buying back the security in the second leg of a repo is equal to the original cash transferred on sale, plus the cost of interest at the 'repo rate'

   See Chapter 3 Section 7.5.2 of your Study Book

2. **B** The IOB auction begins an hour later than the SETS equivalent.

   See Chapter 3 Section 5.1 of your Study Book

3. **A** Whilst all the other options would have an impact on the return to a shareholder, answer A is the most important measure

   See Chapter 3 Section 6.1 of your Study Book

4. **C** Five years is the LSE/FT classification for a short-dated gilt

   See Chapter 1 Section 10.2 of your Study Book

5. **D** A rights issue, as it protects existing shareholders against dilution

   See Chapter 2 Section 5 of your Study Book

6. **B** Where a forward rate quote is at a premium for dollars the premium is subtracted from the spot rate. For the dollar a pip is 1/100th of a cent (the last decimal place of the normal convention). Therefore, the forward rate is

   $2.0375-$2.0385
   ($0.0050-$0.0050)
   $2.0325-$2.0335

   See Chapter 1 Section 20.3 of your Study Book

7. **D** The share capital will only be increased if the warrant is actually exercised

   See Chapter 1 Section 5 of your Study Book

8. **D** As the investor is nearing retirement they should be seeking income, i.e. gilts. Although their pension fund may be low, it would not be appropriate to start investing in high risk investments at this late stage

   See Chapter 7 Section 1.7 of your Study Book

9. **B** Effective control is achieved at 30%, requiring a mandatory offer

   See Chapter 5 Section 1.1 of your Study Book

10. **A** Standard settlement for currency spot trades is two business days after the day of trade

    See Chapter 1 Section 20.2 of your Study Book

11. **C** $P/E = \frac{\text{Price per share}}{\text{Earnings per share}} = \frac{180p}{9p} = 20\times$

See Chapter 6 Section 7.4.2 of your Study Book

12. **D** P/E is current share price divided by latest EPS rather than total earnings

See Chapter 6 Section 7.4.2 of your Study Book

13. **C** Normal market hours on virt-x (the trading hours) are 08:00 to 16:30. When expressed in Central European Time these are 09:00 to 17:30 CET

See Chapter 3 Section 7.1 of your Study Book

14. **D** A reverse repo is a purchase and resale of an asset at an agreed price. Although the date will normally be agreed to, it is the certainty of the price that is more important

See Chapter 3 Section 7.5.2 of your Study Book

15. **A** Eurobonds pay a gross, annual coupon

See Chapter 1 Section 19.1 of your Study Book

16. **B** The vast majority of stocks traded on the IOB are ADRs and GDRs, although the IOB does include a facility for trading equities denominated in Hong Kong dollars

See Chapter 1 Section 5.1 of your Study Book

17. **D** Remember to look at the buy side of the order book if you are selling. Looking at the buy side, there are no buyers willing to pay 159. Since this is a limit order that currently cannot be matched, it will join the sell-side queue above F, but below the other two limit orders currently on the book who were there first

See Chapter 3 Section 3.2 of your Study Book

18. **B** This is the most complete of the four answers available, although even this would not be a comprehensive definition of those securities now trading on SETS

See Chapter 3 Section 1.3.1 of your Study Book

19. **A** This relates to the material/notifiable interest disclosure requirements of the Companies Act

See Chapter 5 Section 2.1.1 of your Study Book

20. **B** ADRs can be traded for up to three months in pre-release form, with the issuing bank required to deposit cash collateral with a third party

See Chapter 1 Section 4 of your Study Book

21. **D** Best execution would be the price matched up first on SETS. Therefore, it would be the best buy (i.e. highest price) and the best sell (i.e. lowest price)

See Chapter 3 Section 3.1 of your Study Book

22. **C** NOMADs are nominated advisers who are approved by the LSE and guide a firm through the process of listing on AIM. They are retained after admission to advise directors on their continuing obligations. It is the nominated broker who helps trade the shares

See Chapter 3 Section 3.1 of your Study Book

23. **C** The UK firm may provide research to the US institutional investor provided dealing is done through a US broker

See Chapter 3 Section 3.1 of your Study Book

24. **A** General insurance covers house, holiday and car insurance, where the maturities of liabilities are much shorter

See Chapter 7 Section 3.1.3 of your Study Book

25. **B** A convertible bond is priced as a straight bond plus a call option. If the underlying falls, the intrinsic value of the conversion right falls and, hence, the convertible bond price decreases

See Chapter 2 Section 5.5 of your Study Book

26. **C** $\text{Price} = \frac{CF_1}{(1+r)^1} + \frac{CF_2}{(1+r)^2}$

$$\frac{£1{,}000}{1.08} + \frac{£11{,}000}{(1.08)^2} = £10{,}356.65$$

See Chapter 1 Section 11.3 of your Study Book

27. **C** Since the ordinary shares receive a dividend, the preference dividend must have been paid for 2007. Since the preference shares are not cumulative, the unpaid preference dividend for 2005 and 2006 is never payable

See Chapter 1 Section 3.1 of your Study Book

28. **B** Only limit orders can remain on the order book. Remember, if you have a buy order, look at what is available on the sell side of the order book

See Chapter 3 Section 3.1 of your Study Book

29. **C** The trade will have been on a cum div basis as the share would go ex-div on Wednesday 14 June. Therefore, as settlement was delayed, the buyer did not get their name recorded on the register by books close date. However, the buyer's broker will be able to generate a claim for the dividend from the seller's broker

See Chapter 4 Section 1.4.1 of your Study Book

30. **D** An introduction does not require marketing, since it is not a way of raising new capital. Instead, it is a way of introducing a new name to the exchange, e.g. following a merger

See Chapter 2 Section 4.9 of your Study Book

31. **D** Profit forecasts are only required in the prospectus for a new issue of securities, not in the annual accounts. The cash flow statement is not a requirement under the Companies Act, but is required under both UK and International Accounting Standards

See Chapter 6 of your Study Book

32. **D** Rights issues are offers to the existing shareholders

See Chapter 2 Section 5 of your Study Book

33. **A** Note that it is this time period that is examinable with respect to the IRS

See Chapter 3 Section 5.3 of your Study Book

34. **C** The DTR Rules say that shareholders must disclose their stakes in public companies when the stake reaches 3%, or for any rises or falls through a full percentage point. Hence, an acquisition of 6% in a public company would need to be reported, as would a disposal for a public company's shares which caused a fall through the 8% percentage point. The rules do not apply to private companies

See Chapter 5 Section 2.1.1 of your Study Book

35. **C** Though an argument could be made for other answers this is a specific feature of CDOs

See Chapter 1 Section 17.4.3 of your Study Book

36. **C** It is possible to split the allotment to take up part of the rights offer and all the other rights nil-paid. However, provided the issuer has complied with the Companies Act requirements, an individual share cannot block the issue

See Chapter 2 Section 5.2 of your Study Book

37. **B** It has the right to participate in profits that are higher than normal

See Chapter 1 Section 3 of your Study Book

38. **D** During a fast market all types of order can be used. A fast market is merely one which involves considerable volumes and/or volatility such that the screen may not be real time but instead lagged. During a disorderly market (when the price jumps >5%) there will be a trading halt, which means that there will be no automatic matching for a period of five minutes. This does not mean the shares cannot be traded, just they will not be matched automatically via the order book. Consequently, limit and market orders can be entered onto SETS and await the start of normal matching

See Chapter 3 Sections 3.3 and 3.4 of your Study Book

39. **D** 00:01 to 24:00 hours is known as the 'business day' and 08:00 to 16:30 hours is known as 'Normal Market Hours' on SETS and as the 'Mandatory Quote Period' on SEAQ

See Chapter 3 Section 3.3 of your Study Book

40. **D** An introduction to the LSE involves introducing shares for trading to the market of the London Stock Exchange for the first time. It does not involve raising cash for the issuing company, since the shares are already held by shareholders

See Chapter 2 Section 4.9 of your Study Book

41. **B** The only obligation is for the DMO to redeem by 2008. Therefore, B is the best available answer

See Chapter 1 Section 10.2 of your Study Book

42. **A** Note that D is talking about PLUS, not virt-x. Large UK and European shares trade on virt-x

See Chapter 3 Section 6.1 of your Study Book

43. **B** This is a description of a cum div trade

See Chapter 4 Section 1.4.1 of your Study Book

44. **B** 100 is the lowest NMS band

See Chapter 3 Section 1.3.1 of your Study Book

45. **B** P/E ratio = $\frac{\text{Share price}}{\text{EPS}}$

$$EPS = \frac{\text{Profit}}{\text{No. of shares}} = \frac{£1.8\text{ million}}{£6\text{ million}} = 30p$$

Therefore P/E = $\frac{360p}{30p}$ = 12×

See Chapter 6 Sections 7.4.1 and 7.4.2 of your Study Book

46. **A** 2½% Consols pay quarterly whereas all other gilts pay six-monthly

See Chapter 1 Section 10.3 of your Study Book

47. **C** The LSE, as one of the RIEs, and the FSA, as the single statutory regulator in the UK, do not represent centralised depositories

See Chapter 4 Section 1.3.3 of your Study Book

48. **B** Add a discount to get the forward rate

$2.0785 – $2.0803	
+ $0.0045 – $0.0048	
$2.0830	$2.0851

Remember that when the bank buys dollars you, as the investor, will get the bad side of the spread, i.e. you will have to give over the higher number ($1.9851) to receive £1.

See Chapter 1 Section 20.3 of your Study Book

49. **A** Revenue expenditure is expenditure incurred in day-to-day administrative expenses, e.g. electricity, telephone

See Chapter 6 Section 4.4 of your Study Book

50. **D** Shares have a ten business day special ex-div period, but there is no special-ex for gilts

See Chapter 4 Section 1.5.3 of your Study Book

51. **A** This is the US definition of a 'qualified' or 'sophisticated' investor by the net asset test. There is also an alternative income test of $200,000

See Chapter 5 Section 3.2 of your Study Book

52. **B** The City Code applies to all UK public companies, both listed and unlisted. It also applies to certain private companies where the company has been listed in the last ten years

See Chapter 5 Section 1.2.1 of your Study Book

53. **A** Committed principal orders must be at least half the normal market size on the ITBB

See Chapter 3 Section 5.2 of your Study Book

54. **A** virt-x is independent of the LSE, has normal trading hours of 08:00 to 16:30 and is order driven, not quote driven. Trades are, however, published instantly

See Chapter 3 Section 6.1 of your Study Book

55. **B** It is the trading of the share on the stock exchange which has been suspended, not the settlement of trades. In this instance the trade has already taken place, so the transaction will settle as usual. However it will not be possible to sell the share on the exchange until the suspension is lifted.

See Chapter 3 Section 3.4 of your Study Book

56. **A** For foreign currency trades, the Bank of England then makes/receives payments to/from the CLS bank. CHAPS is the system by which individual member banks make and receive payments to/from the Bank of England.

See Chapter 4 Section 2 of your Study Book

57. **A** When trades are executed via SETs the central counterparts (CCP) service means that all trades executed on these LSE systems are narrated to LCH. Clearnet. The settlement between LCH. Clearnet and the buyers and sellers will be via CREST

See Chapter 4 Section 1.3 of your Study Book

58. **D** The warrant is at its expiry date and therefore has no time value left. The intrinsic value is £2.00 (the right to buy at £3 when the share price is £5 is normally £2)

See Chapter 1 Section 5 of your Study Book

59. **D**

Spot rate	\$1.9770-\$1.9860
Less: premium	(\$0.0036-\$0.0035)
Forward rate	\$1.9734-\$1.9825

The bank's selling rate for dollars is on the left, since this will give the customer less dollars per £ sterling than the rate on the right

See Chapter 1 Section 20.3 of your Study Book

60. **C** With futures, both the buyer and the seller are obligated unless they have closed out their positions, hence there is risk involved for both parties to the transaction. Option holders have rights, not obligations. However, should they abandon their option, they risk losing their entire investment (the premium initially paid). Small technology companies are seen to be riskier than large, well-established blue chip companies

See Chapter 7 Section 1.7 of your Study Book

61. **D** Stripping this gilt creates the face and ten coupons. All will trade as separate securities

See Chapter 3 Section 7.5.1 of your Study Book

62. **A** The order matching priority for virt-x is the same as for SETS.

See Chapter 3 Section 6.1 of your Study Book

63. **D** It should have been trade reported by 17:15 and thus the senior party to the trade or the seller has breached the LSE rules on trade reporting

See Chapter 3 Section 9.2 of your Study Book

64. **D** For a cum div trade the buyer plays the quoted price plus the accrued interest

See Chapter 1 Section 11.2.1 of your Study Book

65. **D** Preference shareholders always rank higher than ordinary shareholders in a liquidation priority. Deferred shares will rank below these as they have only a deferred right if certain circumstances occur. Warrant holders receive nothing on a winding up

See Chapter 1 Section 17.3 of your Study Book

66. **A** The retained earnings on the balance sheet represents the accumulated profits made by the company since it began to trade, but which have not been paid out as dividends or transferred to other reserves. As such, it is the only distributable reserve

See Chapter 6 Section 3.14 of your Study Book

67. **B** Commercial Paper is a short-term debt, issued at a discount (therefore paying no interest) and normally unsecured

See Chapter 1 Section 18.3 of your Study Book

68. **B** It is possible to refer to medium-term debt as Treasury notes as is the convention in the US

See Chapter 1 Sections 10 and 18.2 of your Study Book

69. **A** The company decides the payment date and book close date. The ex-div date is set by the Stock Exchange and is normally two business days prior to the book's close date

See Chapter 4 Section 1.4.1 of your Study Book

70. **A** ADRs are bearer style instruments (American Form Transfer)

See Chapter 1 Section 4 of your Study Book

71. **A** IOB trades must always be reported to the exchange according to the usual trade reporting rules (normally within three minutes). The publication by the exchange of larger off-order book trades may be delayed by two hours when above four times NMS, and until the next day with above eight times NMS

See Chapter 3 Section 9.3.3 of your Study Book

72. **A** Capital employed = Shareholders' funds + Long-term liabilities

= £10m + £5m = £15m

See Chapter 6 Section 7.2.3 of your Study Book

73. **B** According to the LSE rules, unless otherwise agreed, the settlement will occur in the standard place of settlement for the security

See Chapter 3 Section 5.5 of your Study Book

74. **A** A fixed price order does not exist – it would be a limit order

See Chapter 3 Section 3.2 of your Study Book

75. **A** An index-linked gilt is one where the nominal value of the bond is linked to inflation. The coupon is a fixed percentage, but as it is a real return above inflation it is normally quite low. The benefit that is received at the end is the nominal value of the gilt, which has increased with inflation, and is therefore not fixed

See Chapter 1 Section 15.1 of your Study Book

76. **A** The acronym STRIPS actually stands for Separately Traded and Registered Interest and Principal Securities. Each 'strip' represents a single cash flow. Although only GEMMs can strip the gilts in the first place, once stripped they can be traded on the market. In theory the total value of the component parts should be the same as the value of the gilt as a whole

See Chapter 3 Section 7.5.1 of your Study Book

77. **D** To compensate for lack of income, zero coupon preference shares often carry voting rights

See Chapter 1 Sections 2 and 3 of your Study Book

78. **A** Remember to consider the days from the last coupon (14 May) to the day before settlement (26 June) inclusive (= 44 days). As we use actual day count convention we divide by 365, assuming it's not a leap year

$$£10{,}000 \times 0.05375 \times \frac{44}{365} = £64.79$$

See Chapter 1 Section 11 of your Study Book

79. **B** Although A is part of the role of the syndicate, the underwriting process is simply a 'safety net' in case the syndicate do not manage to pass on the whole issue to their clients. B is the best summary answer to describe the syndicate's role

See Chapter 2 Section 6.5.2 of your Study Book

80. **B** The price must be a multiple of 0.25p as this is the tick size below £5. Therefore, 254.30p is not an acceptable multiple of 0.25

See Chapter 3 Section 3.2.2 of your Study Book

81. **C** Issuing the shares causes an increase in share capital of £5,000 (NV only) and an increase in share premium of £3,000 (excess). Only the share premium forms part of reserves

See Chapter 6 Section 3.4.10 and 3.4.11 of your Study Book

82. **D** A company, its directors and their close relatives will be presumed to act in concert, as will a company and its pension fund, unless there is evidence to the contrary. The fact that the pension fund is a separate legal entity is a legal requirement to protect the members and will be true of all companies' pension funds, so will not be sufficient 'evidence to the contrary'. A company and its employees may be found to be acting in concert but will not automatically be presumed to be doing so

See Chapter 2 Section 6.11.2 of your Study Book

83. **D** A warrant is the right to buy brand new shares in the company

See Chapter 1 Section 5 of your Study Book

84. **A** The Section 793 notice applies to the last three years

See Chapter 5 Section 2.1.2 of your Study Book

85. **B** Share capital consists of **issued** shares only and warrants do not become shares until they are exercised

See Chapter 1 Section 5 of your Study Book

86. **C** Had the question specifically referred to an at best, execute and eliminate, or fill or kill order then the best answer would be 08:00-16:30

See Chapter 3 Section 3.3 of your Study Book

87. **C** The offer must also be for cash in full, or with a full cash alternative

See Chapter 2 Section 6.11.2 of your Study Book

88. **C** This is also known as proprietary trading or 'firm's own' trading

See Chapter 3 Section 1.2 of your Study Book

89. **D** The size requirement for Committed Principal orders is half the Normal Market Size. Orders must be entered within one minute of the end of the opening auction but must be maintained until the end of the closing auction. They can be matched against any of the usual order types from other members, not just limit orders

See Chapter 3 Section 5.2 of your Study Book

90. **C** Gilts have a seven business day ex-div period and therefore can trade special cum during this period

See Chapter 4 Section 1.5.3 of your Study Book

91. **A** Dividend cover is calculated as earnings divided by the net (post tax) dividend

See Chapter 6 Section 7.4.5 of your Study Book

92. **A** Ordinary shareholders rank last in the order of priority on liquidation of a company. They will receive a share of any assets left once all other creditors have been paid. This is not likely to equate to nominal value

See Chapter 1 Section 3.1 of your Study Book

93. **A** There are very few requirements for AIM. There is no history requirement nor minimum free float

See Chapter 2 Section 3 of your Study Book

94. **B** The low-coupon, long-dated bond will be the most volatile and will have the highest duration

See Chapter 1 Section 13 of your Study Book

95. **A** A warrant is like a call option in that it gives the holder the right, but not the obligation, to acquire new shares at a specified price

See Chapter 1 Section 5 of your Study Book

96. **A** Disclosure rules would apply at the 3% level

See Chapter 5 Section 2 of your Study Book

97. **C** Market capitalisation is share price multiplied by the number of shares in the free float. The share price will stay the same but instead of (say) 8 million shares there will be 10 million. In relative terms this is an increase of 25% in total value.

See Chapter 1 Section 8 of your Study Book

98. **D** Debentures are a type of secured corporate bond and, as with all bonds, the investor does not receive voting rights

See Chapter 1 Section 17.2.1 of your Study Book

99. **A** Dividend cover = $\frac{\text{Earnings per share}}{\text{Dividends per share}} = \frac{50p}{25p} = 2\times$

See Chapter 6 Section 7.4.5 of your Study Book

100. **A** The others are all examples of bearer securities

See Chapter 1 Section 2.2.2 of your Study Book

Practice Examination 2

100 Questions in 2 Hours

1. **How many stocks are required to qualify as a portfolio transaction on virt-x?**

   A 10

   B 8

   C 6

   D 20

---

2. **UK corporate bonds may be traded on a special cum basis**

   A For five business days prior to the payment date

   B For ten business days prior to the payment date

   C From the ex-date up to but not including the payment date

   D From the ex-date up to and including the payment date

---

3. **If the US dollar was quoted at a premium of 0.5-0.4 to sterling on the forward foreign exchange markets in the UK, then the forward quote should be**

   A Added to the spot rate

   B Deducted from the spot rate

   C The same as the spot rate

   D Not determinable from such information

---

4. **The gross redemption yield is**

   A The annual rate of return to redemption including coupon payments and redemption payments

   B The annual rate of return to redemption for an investor who pays no tax

   C The annual rate of return to redemption for an investor who pays no tax on coupons (i.e. a basic rate taxpayer)

   D The annual rate of return to redemption for an investor who pays no tax on redemption values

---

5. **ABC wishes to raise funds through a rights issue. The company despatched the rights letter to all shareholders on the register. The shareholder has the right to do all of the following, except**

   A Take up the shares and hold them

   B Take up the shares and sell them

   C Increase his holding by buying additional rights nil paid from the company

   D Do nothing

6. Which of the following would NOT be used by a company raising capital on the market?

A Placing

B Offer for sale

C Offer for subscription

D Introduction

7. A member of the London Stock Exchange

A May deal as principal or alternatively deal as agent

B May deal as both principal and agent

C May deal as principal and quote two-way prices

D May only deal as agent

8. Which of the following are not exempt from stamp duty/SDRT?

A Broker/dealer dealing as principal

B Intermediaries

C Charities

D Market makers

9. Where a person's direct or indirect holding of financial instruments in a company traded on a regulated or prescribed market reaches or falls below 3% of the voting rights, then within two business days, the person must notify

A The company

B The Stock Exchange

C The Takeover Panel

D The FSA

10. What are two other names for a bonus issue?

I Scrip

II Capitalisation

III Premium

IV Rights

A I and II

B III and IV

C II and III

D I and III

11. During a takeover bid, which of the following shareholders of either the target or bidding company must disclose any transaction in that company to the Panel on Takeovers and Mergers?

A Target and bidding company shareholders with 1%

B Only bidding company shareholders with 1%

C Only target company shareholders with 1%

D Target and bidding company shareholders with 3%

12. Which of the following is equal to non-current assets less non-current liabilities?

A Shareholders' funds + Current assets – Current liabilities

B Profit and loss reserve + Share capital

C Shareholders' funds – Current assets + Current liabilities

D Current assets + Net assets – Share capital

13. Which of the following is the requirement for a portfolio trade to be treated as a WPA on SETS?

A It contains 20 or more securities which must all be order book securities

B It contains 20 or more securities of which the majority must be order book securities

C It contains 20 or more securities of which some must be order book securities

D It contains 20 or more securities of which 90% or more must be order book securities

14. How much does an individual need to receive as income in order to be classified as a qualified investor in the US?

A $100,000

B $200,000

C $300,000

D $400,000

15. What is standard settlement for UK Corporate Bonds?

A Two days

B Three days

C Four days

D Five days

16. **The current spot rate GBP/USD is USD2.0375-USD2.0385. The forward quote is at a current premium for dollars of 50 pips. Which of the following is the correct forward rate?**

A USD2.0425-USD2.0435
B USD2.0325-USD2.0335
C USD2.0875-USD2.0885
D USD1.9875-USD1.9885

17. **Which of the following is a secondary market activity?**

A An initial offer of shares on the Official List
B An initial offer of shares on AIM
C A rights issue
D A share buyback

18. **An example of a definitive document of title would be**

A An allotment letter
B A letter of acceptance
C A share certificate
D A confirmation note

19. **Why is investing in preference shares similar to investing in bonds?**

A They have equal security in the event of a winding up
B Dividends on preference shares are usually fixed
C Both must give the same return
D Both have equal voting rights

20. **Which one of the following can be undertaken after the end of the closing auction on SETS?**

A Input of orders
B Deletion of orders
C Automatic matching
D Price advertising

21. **Which of the following can be undertaken during the uncrossing program on SETS?**

A Input of orders
B Deletion of orders
C Automatic matching
D None of the above

22. Which one of the following is not exempt from stamp duty or stamp duty reserve tax?

A Equity market makers buying securities

B Registered intermediaries buying securities and reselling them seven calendar days later

C Gilt-edged market makers buying local authority bonds

D A client buying a new issue in a renounceable form from its original owner

23. The key securities traded on the International Bulletin Board (ITBB) are

A Global Depository Receipts

B US and European blue chips

C US equities

D Asian equities

24. Which two of the following do not trade on SETS?

I FTSE 100 reserve shares

II AIM shares with two or more market makers

III FTSE 100 shares

IV American Depository Receipts (ADRs)

A II and IV

B I and IV

C III and IV

D I and III

25. 4% Treasury 2016 currently has a gross redemption yield of 5.1%. 9% Treasury 2011 has a gross redemption yield of 5.3%. Which of the following investors would you expect to prefer the low coupon stock?

A UK pension fund

B Widow on state benefits

C Company director who earns £50,000 p.a.

D A high income unit trust

26. Between what times will automatic matching take place on the International Bulletin Board?

A 08:00 to 16:30

B 09:00 to 16:30

C 09:00 to 15:30

D 08:00 to 15:30

27. **Dividends paid are shown where in the accounts?**

A Income statement

B Balance sheet

C Cash flow statement

D Earnings per share

28. **When are special-cum bargains in equities permitted?**

A Up to books closed day

B Up to three weeks, following the ex-div date

C Up to the day before payment day

D All year

29. **What percentage shareholding is deemed to give effective control according to the Panel of Takeovers and Mergers?**

A 29.9%

B 30%

C 40%

D 50% plus one share

30. **A convertible bond can best be described as**

A A fixed rate bond and an option to subscribe for a new share

B A floating rate bond and an option to subscribe for a new share

C A fixed rate bond and an obligation to subscribe

D A floating rate bond and a put option to share

31. **Rank the following in order of risk, placing the least risky first**

I Blue chip shares

II Local authority bonds

III Warrants

IV Convertibles

A I, II, III, IV

B II, I, III, IV

C I, II, IV, III

D II, IV, I, III

32. **Trades in Eurobonds must be reported using TRAX within**

A Three minutes

B 30 minutes

C 60 minutes

D 90 minutes

33. How would you define 'return on capital employed'?

A Profit after interest payable and tax divided by capital employed expressed as a percentage

B Revenue divided by capital employed

C Profit before interest payable and tax divided by capital employed expressed as a percentage

D Operating profit divided by capital employed

---

34. Where do French equities clear?

A Eurex

B LCH.Clearnet

C Euroclear

D Clearstream

---

35. The process where a deal manager ensures that, in the immediate market following the issue the price remains above a minimum floor value is known as

A Bookbuilding

B Stabilisation

C Headroom

D Underwriting

---

36. Which two of the following issues raise funds for the company?

I Rights

II Scrip

III Capitalisation

IV Loan stock

A I and IV

B II and III

C I and III

D III and IV

---

37. Which of the following relationships would be true for a gilt trading above par?

A Flat yield > GRY < NRY

B Flat yield < GRY > NRY

C Flat yield < GRY < NRY

D Flat yield > GRY > NRY

38. **Rank the following buy orders in the order they would appear on the SETS order book with the highest priority for matching first.**

	Time	Amount	Price
I	09:03	10,000	186
II	09:15	15,000	184
III	10:08	500	187
IV	09:16	5,000	185

A I, II, IV and III

B III, I, IV and II

C III, II, I and IV

D II, IV, I and III

39. **The current USD/EUR quote is EUR0.6892-EUR0.6945 being USD1 = EUR0.6892 or EUR0.6945. The three-month forward is quoted at 0.92-1.03 (dis). You wish to convert €300,000 in three months' time. How many dollars will you receive?**

A USD426,864

B USD429,553

C USD210,840

D USD209,520

40. **The yield curve is the plot of**

A Spot rates against time

B Forward rates against time

C Redemption yields against time

D Flat yields against time

41. **Where a rights issue is not taken up, which of the following will occur?**

A The company will sell the shares for its own benefit

B The shares will be made available to existing shareholders on application

C The shares will be sold for the benefit of the investor to whom the rights were allotted

D The shares will be cancelled

42. **When does a Eurobond settle in CREST?**

A T + 1

B T + 2

C T + 5

D T + 3

43. Which of the following regarding SETS is false?

A There is no minimum order size

B Market makers set prices within SETS

C Automatic matching takes place between 08:00 and 16:30 on working days

D It is an order-driven system

44. What can the Panel on Takeovers and Mergers do to those who break its rules?

A Public censure

B Fine

C Suspension

D Imprisonment

45. A 10¼% gilt has 18 months to redemption. If the gross redemption yield is 10½% which of the following is closest to the price at which it trades?

A £103.50

B £102

C £98

D £89

46. When will a limit order NOT be undertaken at its stated limit price?

A When exercised during the opening period of the order book

B During the running of the uncrossing algorithm

C When matched against a better priced at best order

D When matched against a better priced fill or kill order

47. A warrant issued by a fully listed public company gives the holder of the instrument

A Entitlement to vote

B Entitlement to dividends

C Entitlement to vote and dividends

D No entitlement to vote or dividends

48. A company has earnings of £1m and five million shares in issue. Its dividend per share is 12p. What is its dividend cover?

A 0.133×

B 0.167×

C 1.67×

D 1.33×

49. For which of these can you calculate the GRY?

A ABC's warrants

B XYZ's Preference shares

C ABC's Step-up bond 2011

D 3-5% War Loan

50. Which of the following is not true with regard to Rule 15A-6 of the SEC relating to a UK authorised firm, not authorised by the SEC?

A A UK firm may solicit business from major institutional investors provided it keeps a written record of advice and trades undertaken

B A UK firm may execute business provided it agrees in writing to be subject to legal and civil proceedings in the US

C A UK firm may not visit a US client without being accompanied by a US broker

D All transactions should be undertaken through a US regulated broker

51. Which one of the following would be included in a company's basic earnings per share calculation?

A Ordinary shares ranking for dividend

B Preference shares

C Warrants

D Convertibles

52. Which is NOT a feature of a T-bill?

A Issued for 91 days

B Sold by auction (tender)

C Have fixed rate of interest

D Are a money market instrument

53. An investor buys some shares just after they go ex-dividend. He shortly receives a dividend cheque from the company. What is his position?

A He is entitled to the dividend

B He is not entitled to the dividend

C He should destroy the dividend cheque

D He should consult his stockbroker on how to proceed

54. Inter-dealer brokers in the gilts market are used by

A Market makers acting as agent

B Market makers acting as principal

C Broker-dealers acting as agent

D Broker-dealers acting as principal

55. **An investor receives a dividend of £3.75 on 225 shares. The tax credit attached to the dividend cheque is for**

A £0.42

B £0.94

C £0.38

D £0.50

56. **The CREST system is**

A A computerised settlement system for UK shares

B A paper-based share settlement system

C A settlement system operated by the London Stock Exchange

D A computerised settlement system for UK shares and UK government bonds

57. **An investor is considering buying a bond with an annual coupon of 5% paid at the end of each year. The bond has a remaining two years to maturity. Current interest rates are 4.25% and are not expected to change over the next two years. Calculate the present value that the bond would be expected to trade at today.**

A £101.41

B £105.52

C £104.25

D £101.21

58. **Which of the following is the best description of the NMS?**

A The service by which investors can pay one another net

B A method for confirming trades executed on OFEX

C The settlement service provided by the London Stock Exchange

D A measure of share volume for a partial or share trade on the London Stock Exchange

59. **On the following SETS screen, which is the best bid price?**

Buy			Sell		
Time	**Volume**	**Price**	**Price**	**Volume**	**Time**
09:41	1,700	755	760	3,500	09:25
09:58	4,300	754	762	1,000	09:15
09:57	1,400	753	763	2,300	10:25
09:57	1,400	753	763	2,300	10:25

A 755

B 760

C 753

D 763

60. A gilt STRIPS market facilitates which of the following?

A Trading the coupon stream and redemption value separately

B Borrowing funds on the security of gilt holdings

C Trading each coupon and the redemption value separately

D The receipt of coupon income gross

61. What is a covered warrant?

A Option to buy shares issued by the company

B Option to buy shares issued by a third party

C Obligation to buy shares issued by the company

D Obligation to buy shares issued by a third party

62. A broker-dealer would undertake which two of the following?

I Buy and sell shares on their own behalf

II Buy and sell shares on behalf of clients

III Provide a facility for anonymous dealing between market makers

IV Quote prices on SETSqx

A I and II

B III and IV

C I and III

D I, II and III

63. With respect to CREST which of these statements is TRUE?

A CREST calculates SDRT on UK and Irish shares at a rate of 0.5%

B Registrars must respond to a Register Update Request within 30 minutes

C CREST members must maintain systems to communicate with CREST

D SETS trades settling via CREST must settle T + 3

64. Which of the following statements about UK T-bills is true?

A They can sometimes be issued by UK corporations

B They cannot be purchased by overseas investors

C They cannot be resold and must be held until maturity (usually six months)

D They are considered to be money market instruments

65. Which of the following is true in relation to forward currency transactions?

A Premiums or discounts reflect expectations of future exchange-rate movements due primarily to inflation

B Forward transactions are only available one month, three months, six months or nine months forward

C The rate at which the transaction will take place cannot be calculated until the currency is exchanged

D A forward currency transaction may be set for any date in the future

---

66. All of the following can be shown as intangible assets on the balance sheet of a printing and publishing company, except

A Goodwill

B Computer hardware

C Publishing rights and titles

D Licences

---

67. If two GEMMs undertake a trade via an IDB the trade report should be made by

A The selling market maker

B The buying market maker

C Both market makers

D The IDB

---

68. What is the best definition of The Bridge?

A Enables communication between depositories

B Enables electronic transfer of securities between Euroclear and CREST

C Enables electronic transfer of securities between Euroclear and Clearstream

D Enables communication between investors and Euroclear

---

69. According to the UKLA Listing Rules, what is the minimum market capitalisation of a company on issue?

A At least £300,000

B At least £500,000

C At least £700,000

D At least £900,000

---

70. What would be the effect of a bond being downgraded?

A Its price would rise and yield would fall

B Its price would rise and yield would rise

C Its price would fall and yield would fall

D Its price would fall and yield would rise

71. Which one of the following would not raise extra capital for a company?

A A 1 for 5 rights issue

B An intermediaries' offer

C A placing of unsecured loan stock

D A 1 for 5 scrip issue

72. A bond paid its last coupon on 7 June, and pays its next on 7 December. How many days are there in the current coupon period?

A 181 days

B 182 days

C 183 days

D 184 days

73. A share goes ex-div on 20 March with Books Close Day as 22 March and Payment Date 14 April. What is the last day that an investor can purchase cum-dividend without engaging in a special cum trade?

A 14 March

B 19 March

C 21 March

D 13 April

74. In which overseas market do Government bonds always settle next day?

A France

B US

C Germany

D Japan

75. Who ranks highest on liquidation?

A Priority creditors

B Fixed charge security holders

C Floating charge security holders

D Preferential creditors

76. Which of the following is not true of Ordinary shares?

A They receive nominal value on liquidation of the company

B They rank below preference shares in the event of a liquidation

C They rank below preference shares in priority for dividends

D They normally carry voting rights

77. If the Stock Exchange suspends dealings in a particular share, which of the following will happen?

A All trading of order book securities will cease

B Automatic matching of order book securities will cease

C Automatic matching and trading of the relevant order book security will cease

D Automatic matching of the order book of the relevant security will cease

---

78. An investor sells Malaysian shares and wants to exchange the proceeds into Brazilian currency. If the currencies are not quoted against each other directly, using what type of rate would the investor be able to convert?

A Cross rate

B Indirect rate

C Implied rate

D Arbitrage rate

---

79. If the LSE imposes a trading halt for an order book security, for how long will this normally last?

A Five minutes

B Ten minutes

C Two minutes

D Fifteen minutes

---

80. A limit order may not achieve the limit price for which of the two following reasons?

I It is matched against a better priced at best order residing on the order book

II It is matched against a better priced limit order residing on the order book

III It is matched during the uncrossing algorithm

IV It is matched against a better priced execute and eliminate incoming order

A I and III

B II and IV

C II and III

D I and IV

81. The following buy orders were on the SETS order book when a sell limit order for 45,600 shares at 457.50p was posted. What would be the gross proceeds for the sell limit order?

Time	Quantity	Price (p)
09:41	10,500	459.00
09:58	25,600	459.00
09:57	800	458.75
08:55	17,855	458.50
10:15	12,000	457.50

A £209,304.00
B £209,258.50
C £54,900.00
D £208,620.00

82. Which of the following is TRUE of an iceberg trade?

A Only part of it is visible
B It may be executed at any price
C It must be executed in full or not at all
D Any unmatched part of the trade will be immediately eliminated

83. A requirement for listing on AIM is

A Three years trading history
B 25% of shares available
C Nominated broker
D Market cap of £700,000

84. Which two of the following are true of ADRs?

I They specify the number of shares that will be held by the depository
II They are American form and therefore not true bearer
III The underlying dividend is automatically paid to ADR holders
IV They can only be traded by US investors

A I and II
B III and IV
C II and III
D I and IV

85. Which of the following is a role of the DMO?

A Issuance of Government debt

B Regulation of the financial services industry

C Regulation of fixed income market in the UK

D Authorisation of GEMMs

86. Which of these is a secondary market activity?

A Rights issue

B Offer for subscription

C A placing

D Sale of a public company to a private customer

87. Which of these is NOT an intangible asset?

A Software licenses

B Goodwill

C Advance payment made to a contractor building a factory

D Trademark

88. When would a trade placed on SETS for >6 × NMS be published?

A Within three minutes

B Within one hour

C Within three hours

D Within one day

89. It is conventional for securities relating to international equity trades to remain

A In country of origin

B In the UK

C In CREST

D In physical form

90. Which of the following is TRUE of GEMMs?

A They must offer firm prices to other GEMMs

B They enter auctions directly with the Bank of England

C They only deal in matched principal to principal deals

D They have an informal, unwritten obligation to buy any unsold bonds during an auction

91. The JGB has a normal life of

A 20 years

B Between 7 and 30 years

C Between 2 and 5 years

D 10 years

---

92. What percentage of shares must a listed investment trust company offer to the public when it first comes to the market?

A 0%

B 15%

C 25%

D 50%

---

93. Which statement best fits the Takeover Code rules?

A Follow the rules of the Code

B Follow the principles and rules of the Code, although the detailed rules may take precedence

C Follow the principles and the detailed rules, however the spirit of the principles may supersede the detailed letter of the rules

D Follow the principles and the detailed rules, unless the FSA requires the FSA principles to apply

---

94. Which of the following statements is false in relation to warrants?

A They are convertible into ordinary shares

B They can be capable of exercise on a daily basis

C They do not carry the right to vote at an AGM

D They must be exercised on expiry

---

95. If a company did a 1 for 1 capitalisation, which two of the following would occur?

I A movement in reserves

II An increase in shareholders' funds

III A decrease in the market price of a share

IV A change in the nominal value of the share

A I and III

B I and IV

C II and IV

D III and IV

96. Which is NOT TRUE in relation to gilt strips?

A Strips can be reconstituted to form a gilt

B An interest component will have a lower value than the redemption proceeds

C Only a GEMM can strip a gilt

D A reconstituted strip will have a market value greater than the underlying gilt

97. Which of the following statements about preference shares is false?

A Preference shares usually carry no voting rights

B All preference share dividends must be paid before any ordinary share dividends are paid

C Preference shares are considered to be less risky than ordinary shares

D They pay a variable annual dividend

98. Which of the following statements best describes the term 'free of payment'?

A The simultaneous transfer of securities and cash in settlement of a trade

B The transfer of free bonus shares to a shareholder entitled to the benefit

C Settlement of a trade which takes place using separate transfers of cash and securities

D The settlement of a transaction by a global custodian which does not incur separate settlement charges

99. A transaction of over £100,000 in nominal value of gilts at 17:15 should be trade reported

A Within three minutes

B By 08:00 the next business day

C By 07:15 the next business day

D Immediately

100. All of the following may be seen on an Income Statement, except

A Current assets

B Revenue

C Tax

D Cost of sales

Answers

1. **A** A portfolio trade on virt-x can be worked for one hour before it is trade reported through to the virt-x system for publication. On virt-x, this is a portfolio containing at least ten different stocks. Do not confuse this with the portfolio trade for a Worked Principal Agreement on SETS where there must be at least twenty securities, of which at least one is a SETS security

   See Chapter 3 Section 6.1 of your Study Book

2. **C** Corporate bonds will trade special cum every day up to, but not including, the coupon payment date. Corporate bonds will trade special-ex five business days prior to the ex-div date

   See Chapter 4 Section 1.5.3 of your Study Book

3. **B** A premium is deducted from the spot rate, a discount is added to the spot rate. A good way to remember this is to look at the numbers in the forward quote – if the numbers decrease when read from left to right, as in this example, then the spot rate is also decreased

   See Chapter 1 Section 20.3 of your Study Book

4. **B** The gross redemption yield is based on before-tax cash flows and ignores income tax on annual coupons

   See Chapter 1 Section 12.2 of your Study Book

5. **C** The nil paid rights would be bought from other shareholders and not from the company. The price paid will be the value of the rights nil paid

   See Chapter 2 Section 5 of your Study Book

6. **D** An introduction describes the process of obtaining a listing for existing shares, rather than raising finance through a new issue

   See Chapter 2 Section 4.9 of your Study Book

7. **B** Acting as both a broker for clients and dealing as principal for the firm is known as dual capacity

   See Chapter 3 Section 1.2 of your Study Book

8. **A** Broker/dealers acting as market makers are exempt since it would be punitive to tax them and, indeed, they would then just be forced to increase their spreads to recover the costs. Broker/dealers trading as principal are required to pay tax since they are treated just like any regular investor. Charities receive very favourable tax treatment. Intermediaries are broker/dealers acting as agents. Although the mechanics of the trade that the broker buys in the market and then sells to the underlying client, the broker is not required to pay stamp duty since the underlying client will

   See Chapter 4 Section 1.6 of your Study Book

9. **A** This is the disclosure requirement for material interest (3%) under the Companies Act

   See Chapter 5 Section 2.1.1 of your Study Book

10. **A** Bonus issues are also known as capitalisation or scrip issues and will enable a company to dilute its share price to improve liquidity

    See Chapter 2 Section 6 of your Study Book

11. **A** Shareholders with holdings of 1% or higher must disclose their transactions. This is in the interest of complete transparency, which is required during the takeover process

See Chapter 5 Section 1.4.2 of your Study Book

12. **C** A rearrangement of the accounting equation where: Non-current assets + Current assets – Current liabilities – non-current liabilities = Shareholders' funds

See Chapter 6 Section 3.2.1 of your Study Book

13. **C** Only one needs to be a SETS security and therefore this is the best available answer

See Chapter 3 Section 3.5.1 of your Study Book

14. **B** This is the US definition of a 'qualified' or 'sophisticated' investor

See Chapter 5 Section 3.2 of your Study Book

15. **B** Corporate bonds settle, like equities, on T + 3

See Chapter 4 Section 1.3.5 of your Study Book

16. **B** Where a forward quote is at a premium for dollars the premium is subtracted from the spot rate. For the dollar a pip is 1/100th of a cent (the last decimal place of the normal quotation convention). Therefore, the forward rate is

$2.0375-$2.0385
($0.0050-$0.0050)
$2.0325-$2.0335

See Chapter 1 Section 20.3.2 of your Study Book

17. **D** A, B and C are all examples of the company raising funds through the issue of new shares, i.e. through the primary market

See Chapter 2 Sections 3, 4 and 5 of your Study Book

18. **C** An allotment letter is sent out when a rights issue is announced and represents a temporary document of title. The share certificate is a definitive document of title but serves only as *prima facie* evidence of ownership. The key evidence of ownership is entry in the register

See Chapter 2 Sections 5.2 of your Study Book

19. **B** The dividend on preference shares is usually fixed, as are the coupons on most bonds, unless of course they are floating rate. Although neither normally carry voting rights, this is not the most important area of similarity for an investor

See Chapter 1 Section 3.1 of your Study Book

20. **B** Once the closing auction is finished, there is an order management period until 17:00 during which orders can be deleted. There is no price advertising period on SETS (only on the IOB)

See Chapter 3 Section 3.3 of your Study Book

21. **D** The SETS system will be working out the common price at which all trades entered during the auction call period will uncross. Therefore, no orders may be added or deleted as it works out the uncrossing price

See Chapter 3 Section 3.3 of your Study Book

22. **D** New issues in renounceable form are exempt from stamp duty reserve tax only to the original owner. If they are then sold the new purchaser is required to pay tax

See Chapter 4 Section 1.6.3 of your Study Book

23. **D** A is true of the International Order Book, B of the International Retail Service and C is a distractor

See Chapter 3 Section 5.2 of your Study Book

24. **A** AIM shares mostly trade on SETSqx and ADRs trade on IOB

See Chapter 3 Section 1.3.1 of your Study Book

25. **C** The company director will be a higher rate taxpayer. He will therefore prefer a low-coupon bond, since he pays tax on the coupon. In addition, a low coupon means that the bond will be trading below par and will therefore have a capital gain which is tax free

See Chapter 1 Section 12.3 of your Study Book

26. **C** Note that these times are different to the normal UK market hours of 08:00 to 16:30

See Chapter 3 Section 5.2 of your Study Book

27. **C** The income statement shows dividends payable, whereas the cash flow statement shows the dividends actually paid in the period

See Chapter 6 Section 5.3 of your Study Book

28. **C** A share can trade special cum any time, as agreed by the parties to the transaction, up to but not including the dividend payment date

See Chapter 4 Section 1.5 of your Study Book

29. **B** 30% is also the definition of control used by the UKLA. (Watch out for reference to the CA 1985 because here control is deemed to be 33.33%.) Option D relates to absolute legal control

See Chapter 5 Section 1.1 of your Study Book

30. **A** Conventionally this is the best description of a convertible bond, although there is no real reason why, in practice, a convertible bond could not be issued with a floating coupon (Convertible FRN)

See Chapter 2 Section 5.5 of your Study Book

31. **D** Warrants are considered the most risky due to their highly geared nature

See Chapter 1 Sections 2, 5 and 10 and Chapter 2 Section 5.5 of your Study Book

32. **B** Eurobond trades must be reported to ICMA via the TRAX Price Reporting System

See Chapter 3 Section 8.4 of your Study Book

33. **C** Interest payable and tax are included for this purpose because they are variables outside the control of the enterprise

See Chapter 6 Section 7.2.1 of your Study Book

34. **C** Euroclear France is the French clearing house

See Chapter 4 Section 1.3.5 of your Study Book

35. **B** The three distractors in this question are all also terms that you need to know. Bookbuilding is establishing the likely price of a new issue. Headroom is the available facility of a CREST Cash Memorandum Account. Underwriting is the process whereby a party agrees to purchase any unsold portion of a new issue for a set price

See Chapter 2 Sections 4.8, 5 and 6.4 of your Study Book

36. **A** Rights issues and loan stock issues raise funds for the company. Scrip issues and capitalisations are another name for bonus issues

See Chapter 2 Sections 5 and 6 of your Study Book

37. **D** Trading above par means that there will be a loss to redemption and, hence, the flat yield will exceed the GRY which adjusts for this loss. NRY is the gross redemption yield net of relevant tax and will, therefore, be lower than the GRY

See Chapter 1 Section 12 of your Study Book

38. **B** The highest buy order would rank first for matching. If two orders have the same price, then the priority is determined by the time of entry, with the earliest order getting priority

See Chapter 3 Section 3.1 of your Study Book

39. **A** The basic rules concerning discount (add) and premium (deduct) still apply whatever the quote, so add the discount to the spot rates. Note that even if the question does not follow the market convention of EUR/USD you must use the rates

€0.6892 -	€0.6945
€0.0092 -	€0.0103
€0.6984	€0.7028

As the investor is selling euros, they will need to hand over more euros to receive the dollars

$$\frac{€300,000}{€0.7028} = \$426,864$$

See Chapter 1 Section 20.3 of your Study Book

40. **C** The yield curve is a graphical representation of the structure of interest rates, plotting the yield offered by bonds against maturity, i.e. the gross redemption yield against time

See Chapter 1 Section 14 of your Study Book

41. **C** These rights belong to the shareholder, hence any 'profit' from selling on these rights needs to go back to the original shareholder. The company will, however, normally take a fee for the sale

See Chapter 2 Section 5.2 of your Study Book

42. **D** Eurobonds settle T + 3, irrespective of whether they settle via Euroclear, Clearstream or the international service of CREST

See Chapter 3 Section 8.4 of your Study Book

43. **B** SETS is an order-driven dealing system for the most liquid UK shares and therefore does not have registered market makers

See Chapter 3 Section 3.1 of your Study Book

44. **A** The traditional sanction is 'cold-shouldering'. However a public censure may be appropriate for less serious breaches of the code. As the Panel has only limited statutory powers, it does not have the right to fine or imprison people. Suspension of shares from trading is within the power of the LSE, not the Panel on Takeovers and Mergers

See Chapter 5 Section 1.2 of your Study Book

45. **C** If the gilt were trading above par then the flat yield would be less than the nominal coupon and would be further reduced by the loss on redemption. This is not the case so the gilt must be trading below par. As the GRY is greater than the nominal coupon only by a small amount and the gilt is soon to be redeemed, it must be trading at only a small discount to its par value

See Chapter 1 Section 12.2 of your Study Book

46. **B** Limit orders may be exercised at the uncrossing price following the uncrossing algorithm

See Chapter 3 Sections 3.3 of your Study Book

47. **D** There is no entitlement to vote or dividends, just a right to buy shares at a predetermined price at a predetermined time

See Chapter 1 Section 5 of your Study Book

48. **C** $\text{Dividend cover} = \dfrac{\text{Earnings}}{\text{Dividends}} = \dfrac{£1{,}000{,}000}{5{,}000{,}000 \times 12\text{p}} = 1.67\times$

See Chapter 6 Section 7.4.5 of your Study Book

49. **C** To be able to calculate a GRY, it is necessary to know the redemption date of the instrument. The preference shares and War Loan have no fixed redemption date, whereas the warrants are an entirely different instrument where GRY would not be an applicable calculation. A step-up bond is one where the coupon rate increases at set points throughout its life. Although this knowledge does not form part of the syllabus, it is the presence of the fixed redemption date which should give the clue as to the correct answer

See Chapter 1 Section 12.2 of your Study Book

50. **A** A UK firm may provide advice to major US institutional investors but may not undertake trades for them

See Chapter 5 Section 3.1 of your Study Book

51. **A** Basic earnings per share is earnings attributable to existing ordinary shareholders only. The fully diluted EPS would take account of warrants and convertibles

See Chapter 6 Section 7.4.1 of your Study Book

52. **C** Treasury bills are issued at a discount and therefore do not pay interest. All of the other choices are true

See Chapter 1 Section 18.2 of your Study Book

53. **B** He is not entitled to the dividend as he bought after the ex-dividend date. He should pass it to his stockbroker so that he can ensure that the correct person receives the dividend to which they are entitled. Whilst answer D is not wrong, answer B is the most accurate and hence the best answer

See Chapter 4 Section 1.4.1 of your Study Book

54. **B** Broker-dealers in gilts cannot use IDBs

See Chapter 3 Section 7.3 of your Study Book

55. **A** The dividend has been received net of a 10% withholding tax. Therefore, divide the net dividend by 90% (0.9) and multiply by the tax rate (10%)

$$\frac{£3.75}{0.9} \times 0.1 = £0.4166$$

See Chapter 1 Section 4.2 of your Study Book

56. **D** CREST also has the ability to settle corporate bonds, some European shares, and also money market instruments

See Chapter 4 Section 1.3.1 of your Study Book

57. **A**

$$\text{Present value} = \frac{\text{Coupon 1}}{1+r} + \frac{\text{Coupon 2 and £100}}{(1+r)^2}$$

$$= \frac{£5}{1+0.0425} + \frac{£105}{(1+0.0425)^2}$$

$$= £4.80 + £96.61$$

$$= £101.41$$

See Chapter 1 Section 11.3 of your Study Book

58. **D** NMS means Normal Market Size, a measure of share volume for a particular share traded on the London Stock Exchange

See Chapter 3 Section 1.3.1 of your Study Book

59. **A** 755 is the best price a seller could receive from a buyer

See Chapter 3 Section 3.1 of your Study Book

60. **C** STRIPS – Separately Traded and Registered Interest and Principal Securities. This effectively creates a market in government-backed, zero-coupon bonds

See Chapter 3 Section 7.5.1 of your Study Book

61. **B** Covered warrants are issued by third parties, as opposed to warrants, which are issued by the company itself. Both warrants and covered warrants confer rights, but not obligations, on the holder

See Chapter 1 Section 6 of your Study Book

62. **A** This is known as dual capacity and applies to all London Stock Exchange members. Item III describes an inter-dealer broker and item IV a market maker

See Chapter 3 Section 1.2 of your Study Book

63. **D** SDRT on Irish shares is 1%. RURs must be responded to within two hours. Only User Members have systems that communicate with CREST

See Chapter 3 Section 3.2.2 of your Study Book

64. **D** UK T-bills are issued by the DMO on behalf of the UK Government and can be freely traded in the money markets

See Chapter 1 Section 18.2 of your Study Book

65. **D** Forward transactions can be done for any date since they are OTC products negotiated between the counterparties

See Chapter 1 Section 20.3.1 of your Study Book

66. **B** Computer hardware is a tangible non-current asset

See Chapter 6 Section 3.4.3 of your Study Book

67. **A** Trade reports are made by the senior party (in this case a GEMM is senior to an IDB) or the seller if both parties are equal

See Chapter 3 Section 9.2 of your Study Book

68. **C** The Bridge links only Euroclear and Clearstream. It is a reconciliation system (enabling electronic transfer) rather than a means of general communication

See Chapter 3 Section 8.4 of your Study Book

69. **C** Shares at least £700,000. If debt is **also** issued it must be for a minimum of £200,000, however it is not obligatory to issue debt

See Chapter 2 Section 3.2 of your Study Book

70. **D** If a bond is downgraded by a credit agency, this will have a negative impact on its price and hence the yield will increase

See Chapter 1 Section 12 and 13 of your Study Book

71. **D** A scrip issue would not raise extra money as it is a capitalisation of existing reserves

See Chapter 2 Sections 5 and 6 of your Study Book

72. **C** The number of days in the coupon period is usually giving to questions relating to clean and dirty pricing. However, in case it is not given to you, you should be able to calculate it as:

Number of days from last coupon date, until the day before next coupon **inclusive**.

In this example:	7 – 30 June	24 days
	July	31 days
	August	31 days
	September	30 days
	October	31 days
	November	30 days
	1 – 6 December	6 days
	Total	**183 days**

See Chapter 1 Section 11 of your Study Book

73. **B** To be entitled to receive the next dividend (without engaging in a special cum trade) it is necessary to purchase the share **before** its ex-dividend date

See Chapter 4 Section 1.4 of your Study Book

74. **B** Make sure you memorise the table giving the properties of different overseas government bonds. Note, whilst BTANs can, not all French Government bonds settle T + 1

See Chapter 4 Section 1.3.5 of your Study Book

75. **B** 'Priority creditors' is a made-up term. Both floating charges and preferential creditors rank below fixed charge holders on liquidation

See Chapter 1 Section 17.3 of your Study Book

76. **A** Ordinary shares receive whatever is left after all other liabilities are paid off. This may be more or less than nominal value. Preference shareholders however would receive the nominal value

See Chapter 1 Section 3.1 of your Study Book

77. **C** Since the share has been suspended it will not be possible to conduct automatic matching or trade it away from the order book

See Chapter 3 Section 3.4 of your Study Book

78. **A** Cross rates enable effective rates to be calculated where the currencies concerned are not quoted directly against each other

See Chapter 1 Section 20 of your Study Book

79. **A** The trading halt will last for five minutes. During this time limit market orders can be input and deleted, and an uncrossing algorithm is run at the end

See Chapter 3 Section 3.4 of your Study Book

80. **C** A limit order will only match off at a better price when it first enters the order book. It will match off at the uncrossing program price if entered during an auction call period. At best orders never reside on the order book

See Chapter 3 Sections 3.1 and 3.3 of your Study Book

81. **B** The sell limit order would be matched against the highest buy offers first

10,500	× 459p	=	£48,195.00
25,600	× 459p	=	£117,504.00
800	× 458.75p	=	£3,670.00
8,700	× 458.5p	=	£39,889.50
45,600			£209,258.50

See Chapter 3 Section 3.1 of your Study Book

82. **A** Only the active peak of the iceberg order will be visible on the order book. Answer B describes at best orders, answer C is a fill or kill and answer D is an execute and eliminate order

See Chapter 3 Section 3.2 of your Study Book

83. **C** All of the other options are requirements to obtain a full LSE listing

See Chapter 2 Section 3.1 of your Study Book

84. **A** As bearer documents, it is not possible for the company paying the dividend to automatically pay it straight to the ADR holder. It is usually paid to the depository where the holder keeps the ADR for onward distribution. Although aimed primarily at US investors, anyone may trade an ADR

See Chapter 1 Section 4 of your Study Book

85. **A** As the sole regulator in the UK the FSA has responsibility for B, C and D

See Chapter 3 Section 7.2 of your Study Book

86. **D** A secondary market transaction involves the sale/purchase of shares which are already in existence. Answers A, B and (usually) C will involve the issuance of new shares onto the market. They are therefore primary market transactions. However, the sale of a public company will by definition involve shares that are already in existence

See Chapter 2 Sections 4.6, 4.7 and 5 of your Study Book

87. **C** A payment made in advance would be a prepayment, included in current assets. All the others are types of intangible assets

See Chapter 6 Section 3.4.3 of your Study Book

88. **A** Delayed publication under a WPA is only allowed when the volume is greater than or equal to 8 × NMS

See Chapter 3 Section 3.5.1 of your Study Book

89. **A** It is just the trading of international securities that will take place in London. The settlement will typically remain in the country of origin

See Chapter 3 Section 5 of your Study Book

90. **D** GEMMs do not have to quote firm prices to each other. It is an Inter Dealer Broker who arranges matched principal to principal trades. Gilt auctions are held by the DMO. As part of their regulatory status as a GEMM, they are expected to assist in the provision of an orderly market for gilts by buying unsold bonds in an auction

See Chapter 3 Section 7.2 of your Study Book

91. **D** The normal life of a Japanese government bond is ten years, however there are some 'superlongs' with a life of 20 years

See Chapter 1 Section 16 of your Study Book

92. **C** A minimum 25% of shares must be offered to the general public as a requirement of the UKLA listing rules

See Chapter 2 Section 2.1 of your Study Book

93. **C** If there is a clash between the principles and the detailed rules of the Takeover Code then the principles prevail

See Chapter 5 Section 1.3 of your Study Book

94. **D** The exercise dates are set at the outset and could be daily and the warrants never carry a right to vote in meetings. A warrant is a right, but not an obligation, to buy new shares and therefore does not have to be exercised at expiry

See Chapter 1 Section 5 of your Study Book

95. **A** A capitalisation issue is another term for a bonus issue. A transfer from reserves (e.g. share premium account) must be made into share capital, thus giving a movement in reserves. A capitalisation issue involves giving the shareholders free shares which have the same nominal value as existing shares. (The term stock-split is normally used when the nominal value of all shares is reduced, i.e. instead of having one share with a nominal value of 100p, the investor is given two shares each with a nominal value of 50p)

See Chapter 2 Section 6.1 and Chapter 9 Section 2.12 of your Study Book

96. **D** A reconstituted gilt should have the same value as the underlying gilt. It is possible that the value could be lower or higher, but arbitrage (buying the cheaper gilt and selling the more valuable strips) would soon bring this back into line

See Chapter 3 Section 7.5.1 of your Study Book

97. **D** Preference shares usually pay a fixed dividend. They are also considered to be less risky than ordinary shares. In the event of a liquidation, they are paid before ordinary shareholders

See Chapter 1 Section 3.1 of your Study Book

98. **C** Free of payment is also known as free delivery

See Chapter 4 Section 1.1.1 of your Study Book

99. **D** It would not be published immediately by the LSE as it is over the £50,000 publication limit for gilts but must, nonetheless, be reported as normal

See Chapter 3 Section 9.2 of your Study Book

100. **A** Current assets appears on the Balance Sheet

See Chapter 6 Section 4 of your Study Book

Practice Examination 3

100 Questions in 2 Hours

1. **Transaction reports for trades executed before 17:15 must be submitted to the LSE using CREST by**

   A 20:00 that day

   B 17:15 that day

   C 18:30 that day

   D 07:15 the next day

2. **What is the aim of the virt-x exchange?**

   A To provide the opportunity for cross-border trading at the equivalence of domestic cost

   B To provide real-time price information on all shares listed in the 12 countries making up the Eurozone

   C To facilitate trading in smaller listed companies from throughout Europe

   D To allow smaller UK companies a facility for trading their shares with reduced compliance responsibilities

3. **The SETS order book for a particular security is as represented below. Your client wants to sell 5,000 of the above shares at 157 worst price. If you place the order on SETS, which of the following statements is true?**

	Buy			Sell			
	Time	Volume	Price	Price	Volume	Time	
A	09:41	1,700	157	159	3,500	08:55	D
B	09:58	2,300	157	159	1,000	09:15	E
C	09:57	1,400	157	160	2,300	10:25	F

   A The order will be matched in full through a multiple fill

   B The order will be placed above order D at the top of the sell side of the order book awaiting matching orders

   C The order will be matched with buy orders A, B and part of C and the unexecuted balance of order C will be eliminated

   D The order will be matched with buy orders A and B for 4,000 and the remainder of 1,000 will remain on the sell side of the order book above order D

4. **Dividends paid are shown where in the accounts?**

   A Income statement

   B Balance sheet

   C Cash flow statement

   D Earnings per share

5. **If a company pays a dividend of 13p for the financial year when earnings were 16p, what is the dividend cover?**

A 1.398

B 0.813

C 1.231

D 0.715

6. **Which of the following statements best describes a fill or kill order placed on SETS?**

A As much of the order as possible should be completed and the remainder should be withdrawn

B The order is completed in full or not at all

C As much of the order as possible should be completed and the remainder left open

D An instruction to deal at a specified price

7. **A bond's redemption yield is 6% with two years to maturity. The coupon is 8% and the bond is redeemable at par. What is the bond's price?**

A £108.00

B £103.67

C £96.54

D £96.43

8. **Which of the following is the best description of a rights issue?**

A A company buying back shares from its shareholders pro rata to their existing share holding in the company

B A free issue of shares to shareholders pro rata to their existing share holding in the company

C An issue of shares to shareholders for cash pro rata to their existing shareholding in the company

D A public offer with preferential treatment for existing shareholders

9. **Why is it NOT correct to say that a bank deposit is risk free?**

A The interest rate may increase or decrease

B The capital may be eroded by inflation

C Capital gains tax may change quickly

D The Financial Services Compensation Scheme may impose a levy

10. **Which of the following is not a heading in the cash flow statement for a company under International Accounting Standards?**

A Taxation

B Operating

C Financing

D Investing

11. Through whom would GEMMs and IDBs settle trades in UK government bonds?

A DMO

B CREST

C LSE

D Bank of England

12. When there is a normal yield curve, which of the following is TRUE?

A A short dated 5% coupon gilt will have a higher yield than a long dated 5% coupon gilt

B A short dated 5% coupon gilt will have a higher yield than a long dated 5% coupon gilt

C Long and short dated gilts with 5% coupons will have the same yield

D The long dated 5% bonds will have a yield in excess of 5%

13. Which of the following yield calculations for a gilt would be most useful for a higher rate taxpayer?

A Flat yield

B Gross redemption yield

C Net redemption yield

D Income yield

14. An investor owns 1% of the share capital of XYZ plc. His wife owns ½% of the same company. Another company, JKL Ltd., of which the investor owns 30% of the share capital, owns 1% of XYZ plc. Which one of the following purchases would require disclosure to XYZ plc under Companies Act legislation (taking each purchase as an exclusive option)?

A A purchase of 1% of XYZ in the name of the investor

B A purchase of 1% of XYZ in his wife's name

C A purchase of 1½% of XYZ by JKL

D A purchase of 1½% of XYZ in the name of the investor

15. How does the Panel on Takeovers and Mergers define a concert party?

A Persons acting together by contract

B Persons acting together by agreement

C Parent and subsidiary companies

D Persons where there is deemed to be a benefit

16. If a company changes its depreciation method so as to reduce the depreciation charge each year, the impact of this is to

A Increase profits

B Reduce profits

C Increase cash flow

D Reduce cash flow

17. For transactions in UK shares on the LSE over £10,000 both parties pay a fee of £1 each. This is to finance the work of

A The FSA

B The Takeover Panel

C The LSE

D The Competition Commission

18. For how long can an order remain on the SETS order book?

A Indefinitely

B Until executed or removed by the member firm placing the order

C For a maximum of 90 days unless matched or removed by the member firm

D The order will be removed if not confirmed by 07:50 on the next business day

19. Who sets the rules for the issuance of new securities?

A LSE

B FSA

C Takeover Panel

D Bank of England

20. If a company has cumulative redeemable preference shares in issue as well as ordinary shares, which of the following statements is true?

A If the preference dividend is not paid this year the ordinary shareholders cannot receive a dividend until all arrears of the preference dividend have been paid

B If the preference dividend is not paid this year then the ordinary shareholders may still receive a dividend next year provided next year's preference dividend is paid

C No more ordinary shares may be issued until the preference shares have been redeemed

D Until the ordinary shareholders have received a dividend no preference dividend can be paid

21. ABC plc has issued convertible debt stock. The conversion rights are 25 shares for each £100 nominal. The stock is trading at £120 for £100 nominal, and the current market price is £3. What is the conversion premium?

A 20%

B 25%

C 33%

D 60%

22. Which of the following is not usually underwritten?

A Rights issue

B Offer for sale

C Offer for subscription

D Deeply discounted rights issue

23. Where an investor has bought a share 'cum' and fails to receive the dividend, having not registered their interest in time, which of the following is true?

A The client's broker will make a claim from the selling member's broker

B The buyer can make a claim directly from the selling member's broker

C The buyer can make a claim directly from the Registrar

D The buyer can make a claim directly from the seller

---

24. You are advising a client as to the risk of the various instruments used by companies to raise finance. Which one of these, in ascending order of risk to the investor, is correct?

A Preference shares, debentures, ordinary shares

B Preference shares, ordinary shares, convertible stock

C Preference shares, A shares, warrants

D Options, underlying equity, warrants

---

25. Under the Takeover Code principles, which of the following is true?

An offeree must not be hindered...

A For longer than is reasonable

B For more than 60 days

C For more than 3 months

D For more than 6 months

---

26. For at least how long must a rights issue remain open?

A 7 days

B 14 days

C 21 days

D 28 days

---

27. A particular preference share in City plc's capital structure is said to be a participating share. Which of the following can be said to be false with respect to this share?

A Extra dividends may be received

B Voting rights are extended if the dividend is in arrears of five years

C Redemption is available at the holder's option

D Income is taxed in the same way as dividends from Ordinary shares

28. A trader places an iceberg order onto SETS to buy 50,000 shares with a limit price of 175p and a peak of 10,000. There is an unmatched sell order on the book with a volume of 4,250 and a price of 175p. Other sell orders are priced at 176p or above. Which of the following is true of the buy order?

A 4,250 matched; remaining 45,750 appears on the order book

B 4,250 matched; 10,000 appears on the order book, 35,750 remains hidden

C 4,250 matched; 5,750 appears on the order book; 40,000 remains hidden

D As there is insufficient volume to match at least 10,000, the whole 50,000 remains unmatched with only 10,000 visible on the book

---

29. All of the following currencies can be used to settle transactions through the CREST system, except

A Euro

B US dollar

C Australian dollar

D Sterling

---

30. Which of the following is false concerning nominee companies?

A Nominee companies are the legal owners of shares held on behalf of customers

B Nominee companies can hold clients' shares in a pooled account in which case only the nominee company's name appears on the register

C Nominee companies can hold shares in designated accounts, in which case the name or code will appear on the register

D Nominee companies are the beneficial owners of shares held on behalf of customers

---

31. Which of the following would be the most suitable investment for a retail client whose objective is to earn capital gains with a low level of risk?

A High-coupon, short-dated gilts

B Index-linked gilts

C Equities

D Zero-coupon bonds

---

32. When would a trade placed on SETS for > 6 × NMS be published?

A Within three minutes

B Within one minute

C Within three hours

D Within one hour

33. If a company does a 5 for 4 bonus issue and the cum bonus price of the shares is £8.00, what will the share price be after the bonus issue?

A £3.56

B £6.40

C £8.00

D £10.00

34. A company with six million shares in issue makes a profit of £1.8 million. Given that the current share price is 360p, calculate the P/E.

A 24

B 12

C 15

D 30

35. What is the name of the payment system used by the Bank of England to ensure that the money transfer will occur for international FX settlement through the Continuous Linked Settlement Bank in New York?

A CREST

B CHAPS

C CHAPSI

D CLS

36. Which of the following best describes an offer for subscription?

A The company issuing shares sells the shares directly to the investors

B The company issuing shares sells the shares to an issuing house which sells the shares to investors

C The existing shareholders in the company sell shares directly to new investors

D The existing shareholders in the company sell shares to an issuing house which sells the shares to investors

37. Investigations under S793 of the Companies Act relate to individuals' holdings of shares over which time period?

A One year

B Two years

C Six months

D Three years

38. For a currency spot contract, when will the currency be delivered?

A The day of the trade

B The working day after the day of the trade

C Two working days after the day of the trade

D Five working days after the day of the trade

39. Which of the following can be used to pay a dividend?

A Retained earnings

B Share capital

C Revaluation reserve

D Share premium

40. An investor receiving dividends on Ordinary share investments, who is not liable to income tax, will

A Be paid gross dividends by the company

B Be paid net dividends but can claim a refund of tax from the company

C Be paid net dividends but can claim a refund of tax from HMRC

D Be paid net dividends and cannot claim any refund

41. Which of the following are trades on the professional currency markets?

I Spot

II Forex

III Premium

IV Forward

A I and II

B II and IV

C I and IV

D III and IV

42. When do UK equities normally settle through CREST?

A T + 0

B T + 1

C T + 3

D T + 25

43. If a market maker executes a transaction after 17:15, by when must a transaction report be made to the Stock Exchange using the TRAX system?

A 21:00 same day

B 21:00 next day

C 22:00 next day

D 20:00 next day

44. What would be the effect of a bond being downgraded?

A Its price would rise and yield would fall

B Its price would rise and yield would rise

C Its price would fall and yield would fall

D Its price would fall and yield would rise

45. Who ranks highest on liquidation?

A Priority creditors

B Fixed charge security holders

C Floating charge security holders

D Preferential creditors

46. When would the opening leg of a gilt repo normally settle?

A T + 0

B T + 1

C T + 2

D T + 3

47. Which of the following is TRUE of an iceberg trade?

A Only part of it is visible

B It may be executed at any price

C It must be executed in full or not at all

D Any unmatched part of the trade will be immediately eliminated

48. The best way to diversify is to

A Pick shares from across the whole market

B Pick shares from one market sector

C Choose shares that are uncorrelated

D Choose shares that are correlated

49. If a company's net earnings yield is 10% and it has a dividend cover of 2×, what is the company's net dividend yield?

A 25.00%

B 20.00%

C 6.25%

D 5.00%

50. When there is a normal yield curve, which of the following is TRUE?

A A short dated 5% coupon gilt will have a higher yield than a long dated 5% coupon gilt

B A short dated 5% coupon gilt will have a lower yield than a long dated 5% coupon gilt

C Long and short dated gilts with 5% coupons will have the same yield

D The long dated 5% bonds will have a yield in excess of 5%

51. A convertible bond is priced at £400 and gives the right to convert into 40 shares. If the shares are currently traded at £5.40 what is the conversion value?

A £12.50

B £7.41

C £291

D £216

52. To be a qualified/sophisticated investor in the US, an individual must have

A Income of more than $200,000 OR net assets of more than $1,000,000

B Income of at least $200,000 OR net assets of at least $1,000,000

C Income of more than $200,000 AND net assets of more than $1,000,000

D Income of at least $200,000 AND net assets of at least $1,000,000

53. A benefit of the LSE's CCP service is

A Reduction of administration

B Disclosure of parties to the trade

C Reduction of FX risk

D Increased credit risk

54. Large UK stocks quoted on the London Stock Exchange can be traded via which one of the following?

A GEMMs

B SETS

C virt-x

D SETSqx

55. To effect a Worked Principal Agreement, which two of the following have to be agreed between the two parties?

I Number of shares concerned

II Price for which shares will be bought or sold

III Basis for selling shares on

IV Type of transactions to be effected after the agreement

A I and III

B II and IV

C I and II

D II and III

---

56. If a client wishes to convert US$1m into sterling and the GBP/USD spot rate is USD1.9850-USD1.9900, how much will he receive?

A GBP1,685,000

B GBP1,690,000

C GBP503,778

D GBP502,513

---

57. For how long prior to books closed day will equity trades through the London Stock Exchange be carried out ex-div?

A 14 calendar days

B Two business days

C Seven calendar days

D Ten business days

---

58. Which of these is NOT an intangible asset?

A Software licences

B Goodwill

C Advance payment made to a contractor building a factory

D Trademark

---

59. Which of the following best describes an index-linked gilt?

A A bond where coupon payments are linked to the rate of inflation

B A bond where coupon payments are inversely related to the rate of inflation

C A bond where the price is linked to the rate of inflation

D A bond where the coupon and redemption value are linked to the rate of inflation

60. If a company acquires 35% of another company's shares and triggers a mandatory bid, what price must they now offer for the shares?

A The most recent price paid

B The maximum price paid during the preceding three months

C Any price they wish

D The maximum price paid during the preceding 12 months

---

61. What term denotes a large trade done through the London Stock Exchange for which the publication will be delayed?

A Bought Deal

B Worked Principle Agreement

C Programmed Trade

D Basket Trade

---

62. An investor purchases £10,000 nominal value of an 8% gilt at a clean price of £102.50 on 5 July. Coupon payment dates are 1 April and 1 October. Calculate the total cost paid by the investor on settlement of the trade.

A £9,830

B £10,040

C £10,460

D £10,670

---

63. Which of the following will be party to settlement of central counterparty trades in UK shares?

I LCH.Clearnet

II London Stock Exchange

III CREST

IV Euroclear

A I only

B I and II only

C I, II and III

D I, II, III and IV

---

64. Free float relates to the number of shares in the hands of

A The company

B The public

C Major shareholders

D Directors

65. A listed company must publish its annual report by how long after its year end?

A One month

B Three months

C Four months

D Six months

---

66. When an investor buys a 7½% Treasury 2010 gilt-edged government security, what does he pay?

A The ex-dividend price

B The clean price plus accrued interest to date

C The quoted price

D The Bank of England's attributed value

---

67. What is the rate of stamp duty reserve tax on UK share transfers?

A ½% on the consideration

B 1% on the consideration

C 2% on the consideration

D ¼% on the consideration

---

68. Which is NOT TRUE in relation to gilt strips?

A Strips can be reconstituted to form a gilt

B An interest component will have a lower value than the redemption proceeds

C Only a GEMM can strip a gilt

D A reconstituted strip will have a market value greater than the underlying gilt

---

69. For index-linked gilts issued after 2005 the RPI used is how many months prior to the coupon date or redemption?

A Eight months

B Six months

C Three months

D Four months

---

70. To which of the following bodies would a company need to apply for its shares to be listed?

A The Stock Exchange

B The Bank of England

C The FSA

D The Treasury

71. If the spot GBP/USD rate stands at USD2.0780-USD2.0785 and three-month rates are 0.32-0.34c dis, how many USD would one need to sell to raise GBP174,000 in three months' time?

A USD362,251

B USD362,129

C USD83,606

D USD83,578

---

72. Which of the following is a requirement to join AIM?

A Minimum capitalisation of £700,000 required

B Minimum track record of three years

C Changes of major shareholdings should be reported

D 25% of shares should be offered to the general public

---

73. Which of the following risks can be eliminated through diversification?

A Market risk

B Systematic risk

C Specific risk

D Systemic risk

---

74. A company undertakes a rights issue at a subscription cost of 75p. If this is a 1 for 2 rights issue and the share price prior to the rights issue was 200p what would be the theoretical value of shares after the rights issue?

A 153.2p

B 148.6p

C 156.2p

D 158.3p

---

75. When two gilt-edged market makers deal via an IDB, they are dealing with respect to each other as

A Principals

B Indirect customers

C Agents

D None of the above

---

76. Companies Act 2006 S793 is applicable to

A Public companies only

B Listed companies only

C Private companies only

D All of the above

77. When a firm holds investments for a client under a safe custody agreement, the FSA rules mandate that

A The firm must segregate the investment from its own investments

B The firm must register the investments held in custody in its own name

C The firm must ensure that no distinction is made between safe custody assets and its own

D The title of the account of the custodian is as anonymous as possible

78. Trades in which of the following government bonds take the least time to settle?

A French OAT

B US T-Bond

C German Bund

D JGB

79. Which of the following is false regarding obtaining a listing in the UK?

A Admission to listing is determined by the UKLA

B The lower the level of free float, the higher the share price volatility

C The minimum nominal value of shares to be listed is £700,000

D The free float should be at least 25%

80. All of the following may be seen on an Income Statement except

A Current liabilities

B Administration expenses

C Tax

D Cost of sales

81. When will a limit order NOT be undertaken at its stated limit price?

A When exercised during the opening period of the order book

B During the running of the uncrossing algorithm

C When matched against a better priced at best order

D When matched against a better priced fill or kill order

82. Who sets the rules for the issuance of new securities?

A LSE

B FSA

C Takeover panel

D Bank of England

83. Which of the following statements is true?

A Pension funds are averse to short-term value risk

B Indexation is a form of passive fund management

C Diversification expands the level of risk that a fund manager takes

D All insurance companies must have at least one ethical fund

84. Settlement of corporate fixed interest securities is how long after the transaction?

A The next business day

B The third business day

C Five business days

D On the settlement day for the relevant Stock Exchange dealing period

85. Who is the central main clearing house for French equities?

A LCH.Clearnet

B Euroclear France

C Clearstream

D Euronext

86. A Committed Principal on the International Retail Service is NOT obligated to do which one of the following?

A Quote firm prices to the minimum display limit

B Quote firm prices during the MQP

C Display firm prices up to display limit outside the MQP

D Actively offer to buy or sell to another member firm at its displayed price

87. Which of the following methods would not be used to price a new share issue?

A Competitive auction

B Fixed price offer

C Tender offer

D Bookbuilding

88. Which of the following is a non-current liability?

A Trade accounts payable

B Tax payable

C Accrued expenses

D Loan stock

89. **All of the following are true of ADRs, except**

A There is a one-off fee on creation of 1½%

B They can be converted back into the underlying shares

C The holder has the right to vote

D Stamp duty is payable by buyers in the secondary market

90. **What is the minimum size for an order to be treated as a worked principal agreement?**

A At least six times the normal market size

B At least six times the publication limit

C At least eight times the normal market size

D At least 75 times the normal market size

91. **What is the price of a share if P/E ratio is 16 and the earnings per share is 21p?**

A 336p

B 373p

C 380p

D 382p

92. **A share is trading with a share price of £5.00 when the company announces a 1 for 5 rights issue at £4.00. What will be the value of the nil paid rights?**

A 17p

B 83p

C 63p

D 37p

93. **A company has a share price of 90p and does a scrip issue so that one new share is issued for every two shares. What will the share price be after the scrip issue?**

A 60p

B 90p

C 150p

D 120p

94. **What is affected by a company's scrip issue?**

A Market capitalisation

B P/E ratio

C Share price

D Gearing

95. Which two of the following are true of warrants?

I An increase in the underlying share price will cause the warrant price to increase

II An increase in the underlying share price will cause the warrant price to decrease

III An increase in the exercise price of the warrant will cause its price to increase

IV An increase in the exercise price of the warrant will cause its price to decrease

A I and III

B I and IV

C II and III

D II and IV

96. An investor holds a portfolio of shares in Rolls Royce plc with a value of £10,000. Subsequently, Rolls Royce undertakes a 1 for 25 scrip issue. Other things remaining constant, what will be the effect on the investor's holding?

A The value will fall

B Unchanged

C The value will increase

D It is not possible to determine the effect

97. Who has overall responsibility in an issue of Eurobonds?

A All of the syndicate equally

B The co-lead manager

C The lead manager

D The issuer

98. If a warrant is priced at £2.50 and has the right to subscribe for £2.00 for a share with a market price of £3.00

A The warrant has a time value of £1.50

B The warrant has a time value of £0.50

C The warrant has a time value of £1.00

D The warrant has no time value

99. A gilt is double-dated 2009-2013. Which of the following is true?

A The investor will redeem the gilt in either 2009 or 2013

B The government will redeem the gilt in either 2009 or 2013

C The investor will choose when, within these dates, to redeem the gilts

D The government will choose when, within these dates, to redeem the gilts

100. Which one of the following would appear on a cash flow statement under 'cash flows from operating activities'?

A Cash paid to suppliers and employees

B Purchase of property, plant and equipment

C Proceeds from sale of equipment

D Proceeds from issuance of share capital

Answers

1. **A** Transaction reports must be submitted by 20:00 the same day if using CREST to report a trade executed before 17:15

   See Chapter 3 Section 10.3 of your Study Book

2. **A** Note that D is talking about PLUS, not virt-x. Large UK and European shares trade on virt-x

   See Chapter 3 Section 6.1 of your Study Book

3. **A** There is sufficient volume of buy orders at the limit price to sell all 5,000 shares at 157. The remaining 400 shares of order C will remain on the order book

   See Chapter 3 Sections 3.1 and 3.2 of your Study Book

4. **C** The income statement shows dividends payable, whereas the cash flow statement shows the dividends actually paid in the period

   See Chapter 6 Section 5.2 of your Study Book

5. **C** Dividend cover assesses whether earnings are sufficient to cover the dividend. If not the company would have to dip into profits from previous years. The calculation is simply:

   $$\frac{\text{Earnings}}{\text{Dividend}} = \frac{16}{13} = 1.231$$

   See Chapter 6 Section 7.4.5 of your Study Book

6. **B** A fill or kill order is, as the name suggests, one where the order is either completed in full ('filled') or not completed at all ('killed'). Option A describes an execute and eliminate order and Option C describes a limit order. A fill or kill order may have a specified price but it is not compulsory to have one

   See Chapter 3 Section 3.2 of your Study Book

7. **B** $$\text{Price} = \frac{CF_1}{(1+r)^1} + \frac{CF_2}{(1+r)^2}$$

   $$\frac{£8}{1.06} + \frac{£108}{1.06^2} = £103.67$$

   See Chapter 1 Section 11.3 of your Study Book

8. **C** Rights issues raise cash and are open to existing shareholders

   See Chapter 2 Section 5.1.1 of your Study Book

9. **B** A difficult question to know what the correct answer is since we are not told which risk we are to consider; interest rate risk or capital risk. B seems to be the best available answer as we are not told that the bank deposit is interest earning (i.e. it could be a non-interest earning or very low unchanging interest current account). It is the purchasing power of the capital rather than the cash amount itself which is eroded by inflation but this appears to be the best answer

   See Chapter 7 Section 1.7 of your Study Book

10. **A** Taxation is a type of operating cash flow under International Standards

See Chapter 6 Section 5.3 of your Study Book

11. **B** UK government bonds (gilts) are settled through CREST, a dematerialised settlement system

See Chapter 4 Section 1.3.5 of your Study Book

12. **B** A normal yield curve shows a lower yield on short dated gilts than long dated

See Chapter 1 Section 14 of your Study Book

13. **C** The only yield measure which reflects tax is the net redemption yield

See Chapter 1 Section 12.3 of your Study Book

14. **D** Connected parties includes spouses but a controlled company requires 33.3% holding. Therefore JKL Ltd is not a corrected party under Companies Act and the investor does not have to include holdings by JKL Ltd

See Chapter 2 Section 6.10 of your Study Book

15. **B** There is no formal contract necessary. Answer C is just one example of parties assumed to be acting in concert, not a definition. D is a distractor

See Chapter 2 Section 6.10.1 of your Study Book

16. **A** Depreciation is merely an accounting entry and has no impact on cash flows

See Chapter 6 Section 3.4.2 of your Study Book

17. **B** This is a levy for the work of the Panel on Takeovers and Mergers

See Chapter 5 Section 1.2.1 of your Study Book

18. **C** Limit orders can only remain on the order book (SETS) for a maximum of 90 calendar days

See Chapter 3 Section 3.2 of your Study Book

19. **B** The FSA, in its capacity as the UK Listing Authority, sets the listing rules. Although the LSE sets its own rules for securities issued on the AIM market, the best answer is to assume the securities are fully listed

See Chapter 2 Section 1 of your Study Book

20. **A** This is assuming the preference shares are cumulative

See Chapter 1 Section 3.1 of your Study Book

21. **D** Effective price of share via the bond = $\frac{£120}{25}$ = £4.80

$\therefore$ Conversion premium = $\frac{£4.80 - £3}{£3}$ = 60%

See Chapter 1 Section 17.5 of your Study Book

22. **D** Deeply discounted rights issues are not underwritten as the big discount in the issue price should ensure that all the new shares are subscribed for

See Chapter 2 Section 6.3 of your Study Book

23. **A** The company paying the dividend will pay the dividend to the registered owner on the books close date. In this case, this will still be the seller even though they traded 'cum div'. Therefore, the buyer's broker claims the dividend from the seller's broker

See Chapter 4 Section 1.4.1 of your Study Book

24. **C** Preference shares have the least risk on winding up. A shares (a type of ordinary share) rank last on winding up, and warrants get nothing on winding up and are geared

See Chapter 7 Section 1.7 of your Study Book

25. **A** This is the term used in Takeover Principle 6.

See Chapter 5 Section 1.3 of your Study Book

26. **C** There must be a minimum of 21 calendar days between the posting of the allotment letter and the last acceptance and payment date

See Chapter 2 Section 5.2 of your Study Book

27. **C** Participating preference shares will receive higher dividends if the company is more profitable. Shares are not normally redeemable

See Chapter 1 Section 3.2 of your Study Book

28. **B** The iceberg order is split into its peaks only after any part that can executed immediately has been matched up. Therefore the order book matches the 4,250 straightaway, then splits the remaining 45,750 into peaks of 10,000. The first of these peaks is therefore visible, with the remaining 35,750 shares remaining hidden

See Chapter 3 Section 3.2 of your Study Book

29. **C** The currencies available to settle with are sterling, US dollars and the euro

See Chapter 4 Section 1.3.1 of your Study Book

30. **D** Registering securities into the legal name of a nominee controlled by a custodian allows the custodian to deal with corporate actions on behalf of the investor. The nominee may operate both a pooled account for all clients and individual designation. However, beneficial interest (i.e. earning income and making capital gains) remains with the customer

See Chapter 4 Section 1.2 of your Study Book

31. **B** The nominal value of the index-linked gilt is linked to inflation. It will almost definitely increase in value and so give a capital gain at very low risk

See Chapter 7 Section 1.7 of your Study Book

32. **A** Since it is a SETS security the answer is A

See Chapter 3 Section 3.5.1 of your Study Book

33. **A** Before 4 shares @ £8

Add 5 shares @ £0

After 9 shares @ £32 ⇒ ex-bonus price = $\frac{£32}{9 \text{ shares}}$ = £3.56

See Chapter 2 Section 6.2 of your Study Book

34. **B** P/E ratio = Share price/EPS

EPS = Profit/No. of shares = £1.8 million/£6 million = 30p

Therefore P/E = 360p/30p = 12x

See Chapter 6 Section 7.4.2 of your Study Book

35. **B** The money is transferred by the Clearing House Automated Payment System (CHAPS) of the Bank of England

See Chapter 4 Section 2 of your Study Book

36. **A** The company handles the entire issue itself

See Chapter 2 Section 4.6.3 of your Study Book

37. **D** Remember, these investigations allow the Company Secretary the power to find out the ultimate owner of the shares. Furthermore, shareholders with 10% or more of the voting shares can also request that a S793 investigation notice is performed

See Chapter 5 Section 2.1.2 of your Study Book

38. **C** Otherwise referred to as T + 2

See Chapter 1 Section 20.2 of your Study Book

39. **A** All of the other reserves are non-distributable

See Chapter 6 Section 3.4.14 of your Study Book

40. **D** The 10% withholding tax may not be reclaimed

See Chapter 1 Section 4.2 of your Study Book

41. **C** Statement II is merely the name used to describe the currency market. Statement III is a method of quoting a forward trade

See Chapter 1 Sections 20.2 and 20.3 of your Study Book

42. **C** Standard settlement for equities is T + 3, three business days after the trade

See Chapter 4 Section 1.3.5 of your Study Book

43. **C** Note the wording 'transaction report' as opposed to 'trade report'. Had the question referred to trade reporting then given this particular trade, the deadline would be 07:45 the next day. Transaction reporting however is required for different reasons (regulatory reasons as opposed to price transparency) and has different deadlines which depend upon the system used to make the transaction report. All trades post-17:15 will have a reporting deadline of the next business day

See Chapter 3 Section 10.3 of your Study Book

44. **D** If a bond is downgraded by a credit agency, this will have a negative impact on its price and hence, the yield will increase

See Chapter 1 Section 19.2 of your Study Book

45. **B** 'Priority Creditors' is a made-up term. Both floating charges and preferential creditors rank below fixed charge holders on liquidation

See Chapter 1 Section 17.3 of your Study Book

46. **A** As repurchase agreements are money market instruments, the person selling the gilts usually needs to borrow money that day so will do immediate settlement (T + 0), rather than the standard settlement for a normal gilt transaction which is T + 1

See Chapter 5 Section 7.5.2 of your Study Book

47. **A** Only the active peak of the iceberg order will be visible on the order book. Answer B describes at best orders, answer C is a fill or kill and answer D is an execute and eliminate order

See Chapter 3 Section 3.2 of your Study Book

48. **C** Shares that are uncorrelated mean that if one goes up in value, the other may not, hence diversifying the portfolio

See Chapter 7 Section 2.1 of your Study Book

49. **D**

$$\frac{\text{Earnings yield}}{\text{Dividend yield}} = \text{Dividend cover}$$

$$\therefore \text{ Dividend yield} = \frac{\text{Earnings yield}}{\text{Dividend cover}} = \frac{10\%}{2\times} = 5\%$$

Note: both earnings yield and dividend yield are net figures

See Chapter 6 Sections 7.4.4 and 7.4.5 of your Study Book

50. **B** A normal yield curve shows a lower yield or short dated gilts than long dated

See Chapter 1 Section 14.1 of your Study Book

51. **D** The conversion value is the current share price multiplied by the number of shares into which the bond can be converted

40 shares × £5.40 = £216

See Chapter 1 Section 17.5 of your Study Book

52. **B** Either of the income or net asset criteria can be met

See Chapter 5 Section 3.2 of your Study Book

53. **A** The identity of the counterparty will not be disclosed, the CCP service has no impact on FX risk, and it reduces credit risk. However, there is a reduction in administration thanks to the ability to settle on a net basis with a single counterparty

See Chapter 4 Section 1.3.2 of your Study Book

54. **B** The FTSE 100 and most liquid FTSE 250 shares trade on SETS

See Chapter 3 Section 1.3.1 of your Study Book

55. **C** The WPA will agree the price and size of the large deal between the LSE member and their client. The LSE member takes the risk of at what price and how they will close out their position

See Chapter 3 Section 3.5.1 of your Study Book

56. **D** USD1.99 is the rate at which the market maker will sell GBP1 (i.e. will buy dollars) so, if a client has USD and wants to convert them into GBP, they will get $\frac{\text{GBP1}}{\text{USD1.99}}$ = GBP0.5025 per USD1, or GBP502,513 for USD1m

See Chapter 1 Section 20.2 of your Study Book

57. **B** The ex-div date is normally from the Wednesday in the week when the books close day is on the Friday

See Chapter 4 Section 1.4.1 of your Study Book

58. **C** A payment made in advance would be a prepayment, included in current assets. All the others are types of intangible assets

See Chapter 6 Sections 3.4.2 and 4.3 of your Study Book

59. **D** ILGs are linked to the rate of inflation using the Retail Price Index (RPI)

See Chapter 1 Section 15.1 of your Study Book

60. **D** The offer must be at least the highest price paid in the last 12 months

See Chapter 2 Section 6.11.2 of your Study Book

61. **B** Categorised as $\geq 75 \times$ Normal Market Size (NMS)

See Chapter 3 Section 3.5.1 of your Study Book

62. **C**

$$\begin{aligned}\text{Dirty price} &= \text{Clean price} + \text{Accrued interest}\\ &= (102.50 \times 100) + \left[(96/183) \times (8\% \times 10{,}000 \times 0.5)\right]\\ &= 10{,}250 + 209.84\\ &= £10{,}459.84\\ &= £10{,}460\end{aligned}$$

See Chapter 1 Section 11.2.1 of your Study Book

63. **C** The trade will have taken place on the LSE (normally via SETS if it is a central counterparty trade), LCH.Clearnet acts as the central counterparty, and settlement will still take place via CREST

See Chapter 4 Sections 1.3.1 and 1.3.2 of your Study Book

64. **B** The free float of a company describes the part of the company in public hands

See Chapter 2 Section 2.1.1 of your Study Book

65. **C** A listed company is also required to produce an interim report which must be produced within two months of the statement date

See Chapter 6 Section 2.3 of your Study Book

66. **B** Gilts are settled dirty. This is the clean price quoted by the GEMM plus the accrued interest to date

See Chapter 1 Section 11.2 of your Study Book

67. **A** SDRT is ½% rounded to the nearest 1p

See Chapter 4 Section 1.6.1 of your Study Book

68. **D** A reconstituted gilt should have the same value as the underlying gilt. It is possible that the value could be lower or higher, but arbitrage (buying the cheaper gilt and selling the more valuable strips) would soon bring this back into line

See Chapter 3 Section 7.5.1 of your Study Book

69. **C** A three-month lag allows the next coupon (six months forward) to be calculated. This is eight months for gilts issued prior to 2005

See Chapter 1 Section 15.1 of your Study Book

70. **C** The UK Listing Authority is part of the FSA, known as the 'competent authority'

See Chapter 2 Section 2 of your Study Book

71. **A**

	USD
Spot rate to buy sterling/sell dollars =	2.0785
Add three-month discount	0.0034
	2.0819

USD2.0819 × GBP174,000 = USD362,251

See Chapter 1 Section 20.3 of your Study Book

72. **C** No capitalisation requirement, no track record and no minimum floatation percentage. An AIM listed company is however required to keep the market informed of important announcements

See Chapter 2 Section 3.1 of your Study Book

73. **C** Market and systematic risk are the same, and relate to the risk of investing in the market in general. This can not be eliminated through diversification

See Chapter 7 Section 2.1 of your Study Book

74. **D** Assume you hold two shares. You will be given the right to buy one new share

	Number of Shares	Current Price	Total
Before or cum-rights price	2	£2.00	£4.00
Rights price	1	£0.75	£0.75
After or ex-rights price	3	X	£4.75

Therefore, theoretical ex-rights price is £4.75/3 = 158.3 pence

See Chapter 2 Section 5.3.1 of your Study Book

75. **D** They are both dealing as principals with the IDB, not with each other

See Chapter 3 Section 7 of your Study Book

76. **A** S793 of CA2006 gives the Company Secretary of a **public company** the power to require shareholders to give information. The investigation notice can be sent to existing shareholders, asking them to reveal the ultimate owner of any shares held in their name, or to a particular individual asking whether he has in the last three years been a direct or indirect shareholder in the company

See Chapter 5 Section 2.1.2 of your Study Book

77. **A** All the other alternatives would breach the rule on segregation

See Chapter 1 Section 4.2 of your Study Book

78. **B** US government bonds settle T + 1. The French, German and JGB settle T + 3

See Chapter 4 Section 1.3.5 of your Study Book

79. **C** If fewer shares are issued to the public (lower free float) then the share will be less liquid giving rise to bigger share price fluctuation (higher volatility). It is the minimum **market** value not nominal value which must be at least £700,000

See Chapter 3 Section 3.2 of your Study Book

80. **A** Current liabilities appear on the Balance Sheet

See Chapter 6 Sections 3.2.3 and 4.2 of your Study Book

81. **B** Limit orders may be exercised at the uncrossing price following the uncrossing algorithm

See Chapter 3 Section 3.3 of your Study Book

82. **B** The FSA, in its capacity as the UK Listing Authority, sets the listing rules. Although the LSE sets its own rules for securities issued on the AIM market, the best answer is to assume the securities are fully listed

See Chapter 2 Section 2 of your Study Book

83. **B**
   - A Pension funds may take short-term risks as their investment objectives are long term
   - B Tracking an index, e.g. FTSE 100 is passive fund management
   - C Diversification reduces risk by spreading a fund over more investments
   - D There is no requirement to have an ethical fund

See Chapter 7 Sections 2 and 3 of your Study Book

84. **B** Most securities settle T + 3. It is often easier to learn those that do not settle T + 3: Gilts, US T-bonds and nil-paid rights all settle T + 1; spot currency settles T + 2

See Chapter 4 Section 1.3.5 of your Study Book

85. **B** Euroclear France is the correct answer

See Chapter 14 Section 1.3.5 of your Study Book

86. **C** Market makers (also known as Committed Principals) are only required to display firm prices during the Mandatory Quote Period

See Chapter 3 Section 5.3 of your Study Book

87. **A** The basic premise of a new share issue is that all participants pay the same price. With a competitive auction, successful bidders would pay the price that they bid

See Chapter 2 Section 4.8 of your Study Book

88. **D** All of the others are classed as current liabilities

See Chapter 6 Section 3.4.7 of your Study Book

89. **D** There is no stamp duty on ADRs when traded, hence the 1½% fee charges on creation

See Chapter 1 Section 4 of your Study Book

90. **C** The requirement is $\geq 8 \times$ NMS

See Chapter 3 Section 3.5.1 of your Study Book

91. **A** Price per share/Earnings per share = 16

Therefore Price per share = Earnings per share × 16 = 21p × 16 = 336p

See Chapter 6 Section 7.4.2 of your Study Book

92. **B** Let's say that before the offering a shareholder has five shares. His shares are worth £4.83 (theoretical ex-rights price). The nil paid rights price is therefore £4.83 – £4.00 = 83p

See Chapter 2 Section 5.3.2 of your Study Book

93. **A**

Before	2	×	90p	=	180p
Add	1	×	FREE	=	–
After	3				180p

Ex-bonus price = $\frac{180p}{3} = 60p$

See Chapter 2 Section 6.2 of your Study Book

94. **C** Reserves are made into new shares and no new funds are raised for the company. Share price is reduced as a consequence

See Chapter 2 Section 6.1 of your Study Book

95. **B** An increase in the underlying will make the right to buy at the same fixed price more attractive. However, an increase in the exercise price for buying the same asset will make it less attractive

See Chapter 1 Section 5 of your Study Book

96. **B** The ex-bonus price will fall but not the total value of the total holding

See Chapter 2 Section 6.1 of your Study Book

97. **C** The lead manager is given the power and responsibility to issue the bond on behalf of the issuers. Although they often create a syndicate and have a co-lead manager to help them to market the issue, the ultimate responsibility lies with the lead manager

See Chapter 2 Section 6.5.2 of your Study Book

98. **A** Intrinsic value = Market price – Subscription price (£3 – £2 = £1)

Time value = Warrant price – Intrinsic value (£2.50 – £1 = £1.50)

See Chapter 1 Section 5 of your Study Book

99. **D** The government will choose when within these dates to redeem – the earliest being 2009 and the latest being 2013

See Chapter 1 Section 10.2 of your Study Book

100. **A** B and C appear under 'cash flow from investment activities' and D from 'cash flows from financing activities'

See Chapter 6 Section 5.3 of your Study Book